TARGE
MATHS

Year 4

Stephen Pearce

Elmwood Press

© Stephen Pearce

First published 2002 by
Elmwood Press
80 Attimore Road
Welwyn Garden City
Herts. AL8 6LP
Tel. 01707 333232
Reprinted 2003, 2004, 2005, 2007

British Library Cataloguing in Publication Data

Pearce, Stephen

    1. Mathematics—1961–
    I. Title

    ISBN 1 902 214 226

Numerical answers are published in a separate book

Typeset and illustrated by Tech-Set Ltd., Gateshead, Tyne and Wear
Printed and bound by WS Bookwell.

PREFACE

Target Maths has been written for pupils in Year 4 and their teachers.

The intention of the book is to provide teachers with material to teach *all* the NNS objectives, as set out in the yearly teaching programme, with *all* the children in their class able to work at their appropriate level of ability.

One of the key principles for the approach to teaching recommended by the NNS is 'controlled differentiation, with all pupils engaged in mathematics related to a common theme.' **Target Maths** is structured so that controlled differentiation is built into every lesson. How a teacher decides to use the material would depend upon the children's familiarity with the topic and the amount of time available.

Each lesson in the book is divided into four sections. The four sections are:

- The introduction: a clearly stated learning intention and, where necessary, explanations and examples of new work.
- Section A: activities based upon the NNS expected learning outcomes for Year 3 pupils. This section can be used to remind children of work previously covered, as well as providing material for the less confident child.
- Section B: activities based upon the NNS expected learning outcomes for Year 4 pupils. Most children should be able to work successfully at this level.
- Section C: activities based upon the NNS expected learning outcomes for Year 5 pupils. This section provides extension material for the faster workers and for those who need to be moved quickly onto more challenging tasks. Problems in Section C can also provide useful material for discussion in the plenary session.

The correspondence of the three sections to the NNS learning outcomes expected of different year groups provides a simple, manageable framework for both the formal and informal assessment of children's progress. The expectations in the yearly teaching programmes correspond to these National Curriculum levels.

- Section A   Year 3   revision of level 2, but mainly level 3
- Section B   Year 4   consolidation of level 3, and start on level 4
- Section C   Year 5   revision of level 3, but mainly level 4

Both the NNS Teaching Programme for Year 4 and the Term Framework are in the Answer Book with **Target Maths** page references for all the NNS objectives.

The author is indebted to many colleagues who have assisted him in this work. He is particularly grateful to David Rayner and Sharon Granville for their invaluable advice and support.

CONTENTS

On these pages you will learn to read and write whole numbers.

Numbers are made up from digits.

There are ten digits: 0, 1, 2, 3, 4, 5, 6, 7, 8 and 9.
3 is a single digit number, 32 is a two-digit number, and so on.

The way we read a digit depends upon its place in the number.
274 is read as two hundred and seventy-four.
2748 is read as two thousand seven hundred and forty-eight.

TAKE CARE when a number has noughts in it.
3060 is read as three thousand and sixty.
3006 is read as three thousand and six.

A

Copy the table, writing each distance in figures.

Place	Road distance to London (kilometres)
1 Lincoln	two hundred and eleven
2 Bristol	one hundred and ninety-six
3 Leeds	three hundred and four
4 Aberdeen	eight hundred and thirty-two
5 Land's End	four hundred and seventy-eight
6 Manchester	two hundred and ninety-eight
7 Edinburgh	six hundred and twenty-eight
8 Cardiff	two hundred and fifty-three
9 Penzance	five hundred and fifteen
10 Nottingham	two hundred and nine

These figures also show the distance between London and other places by road. Write each distance in words.

11	Birmingham	188 km	16	Cambridge	87 km
12	Exeter	291 km	17	Inverness	885 km
13	Liverpool	325 km	18	Gloucester	639 km
14	Newcastle	460 km	19	Blackpool	364 km
15	York	333 km	20	Dundee	721 km

B

Copy the table, writing each distance in figures.

1

River	Length (kilometres)
Amazon	six thousand seven hundred and fifty
Nile	six thousand six hundred and seventy
Yangtze	six thousand three hundred
Mississippi	six thousand and twenty
Yenisey	five thousand five hundred and forty
Hwang He	five thousand four hundred and sixty-four
Ob	five thousand four hundred and nine
Parana	four thousand eight hundred and eighty
Congo	four thousand seven hundred
Lena	four thousand four hundred

The figures below give the lengths of the same rivers in miles. Write each distance in words.

2 Amazon   4194 miles

3 Nile   4145 miles

4 Yangtze   3915 miles

5 Mississippi   3741 miles

6 Yenisey   3442 miles

7 Hwang He   3395 miles

8 Ob   3361 miles

9 Parana   3032 miles

10 Congo   2920 miles

11 Lena   2734 miles

C

One thousand thousands is one million. (1 000 000).

Copy these sentences writing the numbers in figures.

1 The Moon is about a quarter of a million miles from the Earth.

2 The population of Sheffield is about half of a million.

3 One tenth of a million people watched the football match.

4 Kieran won three quarters of a million pounds on the Lottery.

5 Use the digits on the cards.
Make as many five-digit numbers as you can with
a value of between 25 000 and 28 000.
Write each number:
a) in figures   b) in words.

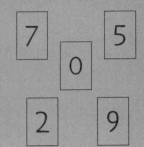

On this page you will learn to know what each digit in a number represents and how to partition numbers.

Example

Th	H	T	U
3	6	9	8

The 3 has a value of 3000.
The 6 has a value of 600.
The 9 has a value of 90.
The 8 has a value of 8 units.

Knowing the value of the digits means that you are able to partition numbers.

Example $3698 = 3000 + 600 + 90 + 8$

A

Copy and complete by writing the missing number in the box.

1 $128 = 100 + 20 + \square$

2 $369 = 300 + \square + 9$

3 $427 = \square + 20 + 7$

4 $584 = 500 + \square + 4$

5 $392 = \square + 90 + 2$

6 $655 = 600 + 50 + \square$

7 $716 = 700 + \square + 6$

8 $925 = \square + 20 + 5$

9 $821 = 800 + \square + \square$

10 $442 = \square + \square + 2$

11 $673 = \square + 70 + \square$

12 $739 = \square + \square + \square$

Write down the value of the digit underlined.

13 3<u>2</u>8   19 7<u>1</u>4

14 17<u>9</u>   20 <u>3</u>07

15 <u>8</u>46   21 93<u>8</u>

16 5<u>8</u>5   22 6<u>9</u>2

17 <u>4</u>51   23 <u>2</u>60

18 3<u>6</u>2   24 51<u>3</u>

B

What is the value of the digit underlined.

1 2<u>3</u>6   10 2<u>5</u>6

2 <u>5</u>47   11 <u>4</u>444

3 <u>2</u>184   12 80<u>7</u>0

4 439<u>5</u>   13 <u>3</u>29

5 1<u>6</u>38   14 <u>3</u>463

6 54<u>4</u>0   15 798<u>5</u>

7 <u>7</u>063   16 10<u>3</u>0

8 492<u>2</u>   17 1<u>2</u>6

9 <u>9</u>648   18 2<u>7</u>51

Partition these numbers as in the example.

19 1627   23 4538

20 2452   24 5843

21 3985   25 7296

22 2174   26 8310

Copy and complete

27 $2594 = 2000 + \square + 94$

28 $1635 = 1600 + \square$

29 $389 = 300 + \square$

30 $8194 = 8000 + \square$

31 $6523 = \square + 523$

32 $1277 = \square + 77$

33 $4718 = 4000 + \square$

34 $2156 = 2000 + \square + 6$

C

Take 50 from: Add 600 to:

1 6187   6 2317

2 573   7 169

3 1258   8 5034

4 4760   9 27

5 991.   10 8.

Take 200 from: Add 600 to:

11 814   16 1279

12 3636   17 815

13 5380   18 36

14 742   19 5423

15 2475.   20 2840.

What needs to be added or subtracted to change:

21 382 to 352

22 2794 to 2294

23 1068 to 7068

24 4856 to 4456

25 7321 to 9321

26 1627 to 1697

27 5340 to 5840

28 8915 to 3915

29 6218 to 6298

30 2831 to 2231.

On this page you will learn:

• to multiply whole numbers by 10.
Move the digits one place to the left and add a nought to the units column.

Examples $6 \times 10 = 60$ $62 \times 10 = 620$ $624 \times 10 = 6240$

• to divide whole numbers by 10.
Move the digits one place to the right.

Examples $3700 \div 10 = 370$ $370 \div 10 = 37$ $30 \div 10 = 3$

A

Work out

1 4×10 9 5×10

2 7×10 10 91×10

3 9×10 11 60×10

4 8×10 12 73×10

5 16×10 13 2×10

6 20×10 14 50×10

7 38×10 15 67×10

8 52×10 16 100×10

Work out

17 $20 \div 10$ 25 $590 \div 10$

18 $30 \div 10$ 26 $400 \div 10$

19 $50 \div 10$ 27 $770 \div 10$

20 $100 \div 10$ 28 $840 \div 10$

21 $700 \div 10$ 29 $300 \div 10$

22 $140 \div 10$ 30 $560 \div 10$

23 $240 \div 10$ 31 $1000 \div 10$

24 $60 \div 10$ 32 $410 \div 10$

How many 10p's make:

33 £1   36 £12

34 £5   37 £3

35 £10   38 £20?

B

Multiply by 10.

1 176   7 430

2 49   8 835

3 578   9 701

4 300   10 37

5 224   11 150

6 6   12 467

Divide by 10.

13 8000   19 7550

14 2160   20 4090

15 570   21 9360

16 3640   22 5000

17 1480   23 2720

18 3200   24 6400

Copy and complete.

25 ☐ $\times 10 = 630$

26 $280 \ ☐ \ 10 = 28$

27 ☐ $\times 10 = 6280$

28 ☐ $\div 10 = 239$

29 $565 \ ☐ \ 10 = 5650$

30 ☐ $\div 10 = 37$

31 $8400 \ ☐ \ 10 = 840$

32 ☐ $\times 10 = 210$

C

Work out

1 386×10

2 $6320 \div 10$

3 7×100

4 $600 \div 100$

5 947×10

6 $10\,000 \div 10$

7 14×100

8 $1700 \div 100$

9 2000×10

10 $12\,500 \div 10$

11 43×100

12 $2500 \div 100$

How many 10p's make:

13 £30   16 £2000

14 £180   17 £700

15 £68   18 £1430?

How many 1p's make:

19 £5   22 £360

20 £400   23 £90

21 £23   24 £1000?

How many cm's make:

25 1 m   27 17 m

26 8 m   28 100 m?

On these pages you will learn to count on and back in 1s, 10s and 100s.

Examples

Count on 6 in 1s from 728.

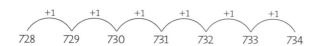

Count back 60 in 10s from 728.

Count on 600 in 100s from 728.

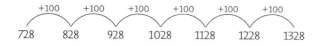

Count back 6000 in 1000s from 7280.

```
  −1000  −1000  −1000  −1000  −1000  −1000
7280   6280   5280   4280   3280   2280   1280
```

Count on 6000 from 3540.

```
  +1000  +1000  +1000  +1000  +1000  +1000
3540   4540   5540   6540   7540   8540   9540
```

A

Count on in 1s.
1 6 from 564
2 4 from 831
3 9 from 796
4 12 from 408

Count back in 1s.
5 5 from 212
6 7 from 564
7 11 from 935
8 8 from 307

Count on in 10s.
9 60 from 356
10 40 from 783
11 70 from 460
12 80 from 849

Count back in 10s.
13 50 from 342
14 80 from 520
15 60 from 635
16 90 from 479

Count on in 100s.
17 400 from 583
18 600 from 266
19 500 from 314
20 700 from 197

Count back in 100s.
21 300 from 681
22 400 from 578
23 700 from 724
24 600 from 917

Copy and complete by writing the missing numbers in the boxes.

25 246 247 248 249 ☐ ☐ ☐
26 658 668 678 688 ☐ ☐ ☐
27 551 541 531 521 ☐ ☐ ☐
28 879 779 679 579 ☐ ☐ ☐
29 385 384 383 382 ☐ ☐ ☐
30 367 377 387 397 ☐ ☐ ☐
31 446 436 426 416 ☐ ☐ ☐
32 235 335 435 535 ☐ ☐ ☐

B

Count on in 10s.

1. 50 from 282
2. 80 from 467
3. 60 from 741
4. 70 from 955

Count back in 1s.

5. 5 from 357
6. 6 from 274
7. 7 from 638
8. 8 from 495

Count on in 100s.

9. 400 from 1812
10. 700 from 1764
11. 500 from 3635
12. 800 from 2790

Count back in 10s.

13. 40 from 523
14. 50 from 130
15. 60 from 952
16. 80 from 726

Count on in 1000s.

17. 3000 from 1271
18. 5000 from 3952
19. 4000 from 2503
20. 7000 from 3487

Count back in 100s.

21. 300 from 2165
22. 600 from 3587
23. 500 from 1240
24. 700 from 7391

Add 10 to:

25. 538
26. 279
27. 165
28. 421.

Add 100 to:

29. 4210
30. 3587
31. 2941
32. 5756.

Add 1000 to:

33. 2491
34. 6580
35. 374
36. 7900.

Take 10 from:

37. 762
38. 413
39. 359
40. 806.

Take 100 from:

41. 3261
42. 5694
43. 4170
44. 2808.

Take 1000 from:

45. 2678
46. 5301
47. 4814
48. 1453.

C

Copy and complete the calculation squares.

1

+	100	10	1	1000
1697	1797			
399				
2914		2924		
4979				

2

−	10	100	1000	1
3210		3110		
1398				
2107				2106
4052				

Add 30 to:

3. 365
4. 1258
5. 2381.

Start at 479.

18. +1
19. +100
20. +1000

Add 200 to:

6. 869
7. 1437
8. 2917.

Start at 1203.

21. −100
22. −10
23. −1000

Take 20 from:

9. 1367
10. 814
11. 1605.

Start at 5309.

24. +10
25. +1
26. +1000

Take 300 from:

12. 5416
13. 1230
14. 7001.

Start at 2999.

27. +1
28. +10
29. +100

Take 2000 from:

15. 8029
16. 5182
17. 2360.

Start at 4000.

30. −1
31. −10
32. −100

On these pages you will learn:

- **to use the symbols <, > and ×.**

  > means 'is greater than'.
  < means 'is less than'.
  = means 'is equal to'.

- **to work out the number lying half way between two other numbers.**

Example

Find the number half way between 6200 and 6800.

Find the difference between the numbers.
6800 − 6200 = 600

Work out half the difference.
600 ÷ 2 = 300

Add half the difference to the lower number.
6200 + 300 = 6500

- **to order a set of numbers in order of size.**

Example

2581   2158   21158
Put these numbers in order with the largest first.

The 2 in 21158 has a value of 20 000 and is the highest value digit.

The 2s in 2581 and 2158 both have a value of 2000.

The 5 in 2581 is the second digit with the highest value in that pair of numbers.

Therefore the order is: 21158   2581   2158.

A

Which number is smaller?
1. 68 or 86
2. 93 or 39
3. 351 or 315
4. 428 or 482
5. 267 or 276
6. 195 or 159
7. 345 or 354
8. 781 or 718

Which number is larger?
9. 34 or 43
10. 89 or 98
11. 932 or 923
12. 548 or 584
13. 126 or 162
14. 654 or 645
15. 432 or 423
16. 278 or 287

Put these sets of numbers in order starting with the smallest.
17. 382   283   823   238
18. 714   417   174   471
19. 325   532   523   352
20. 649   469   496   694

Find the number that is halfway on each of these number lines.
21. 210 ⊢——————┴——————⊣ 220
22. 95 ⊢——————┴——————⊣ 105
23. 500 ⊢——————┴——————⊣ 600
24. 300 ⊢——————┴——————⊣ 310

Answer 'True' or 'False'.
25. 62 > 26
26. 308 < 380
27. 10 × 8 > 3 × 30
28. Half of 100 < 5 × 10

B

Copy and complete by putting <, > or = in the box.

1. $7 \times 2 \square 2 \times 5$
2. $8 \times 3 \square 4 \times 6$
3. $6 \times 4 \square 5 \times 5$

4. $3 \times 6 \square 9 \times 2$
5. $5 \times 7 \square 6 \times 6$
6. $10 \times 6 \square 15 \times 3$

7. $8 \times 4 \square 7 \times 5$
8. $7 \times 3 \square 5 \times 4$
9. $5 \times 8 \square 10 \times 4$

10. $6 \times 3 \square 4 \times 5$
11. $10 \times 9 \square 45 \times 2$
12. $9 \times 4 \square 5 \times 7$

Put these numbers in order, starting with the largest.

13. 2635   3256   2536   3526
14. 1984   1849   1498   4189
15. 6472   7462   6724   7246
16. 3748   3874   3784   3478
17. 1546   1654   1456   1465
18. 3187   3781   3871   3817

Find the number that is halfway on each of these number lines.

19. 1300 |____|____| 1310
20. 550 |____|____| 600
21. 2000 |____|____| 2100
22. 150 |____|____| 250
23. 1360 |____|____| 1400
24. 1900 |____|____| 2000

C

Copy and complete by putting <, > or = in the box.

1. $7 \times 6 \square 8 \times 5$
2. $9 \times 6 \square 14 \times 4$
3. $6 \times 9 \square 27 \times 2$

4. $7 \times 8 \square 3 \times 18$
5. $8 \times 6 \square 4 \times 12$
6. $8 \times 9 \square 3 \times 25$

7. $9 \times 9 \square 4 \times 20$
8. $6 \times 8 \square 7 \times 7$
9. $6 \times 7 \square 14 \times 3$

10. $7 \times 7 \square 25 \times 2$
11. $9 \times 8 \square 3 \times 24$
12. $8 \times 7 \square 11 \times 5$

13. Use these digits once each.
    Make two 3-digit numbers which give:

    2 5 9 3 4 7

    a) the largest possible total.
    b) the smallest possible total.
    c) the largest possible difference.
    d) the smallest possible difference.

Work out the number that is halfway between these numbers.

14. 3460 ⟷ 3660
15. 2000 ⟷ 2500
16. 4530 ⟷ 4610
17. 19500 ⟷ 21500
18. 950 ⟷ 1050
19. 2095 ⟷ 2125
20. 1440 ⟷ 1500
21. 17280 ⟷ 17290

On these pages you will learn to make and justify estimates.

A

Estimate the numbers shown by the arrows.

1

2

3

4

5

6

7 Estimate the number of dots in the large square. Do not count them. Explain your method.

8 Estimate how many stacked copies of this book would reach 1 m high. Use your method to estimate how many stacked copies of other books would reach 1 m high.

B

Estimate the numbers shown by the arrows.

1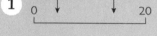

2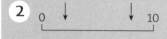

3

4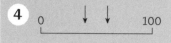

5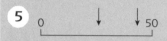

6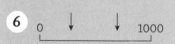

7 Class 4 collected the rainfall each day.

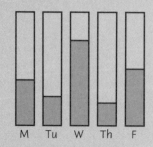

On which day was there:
a) three times as much rainfall as on Tuesday?
b) double the rainfall that fell on Thursday?
c) half the Friday rainfall?

C

Estimate the numbers shown by the arrows.

1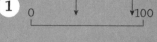

2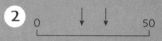

3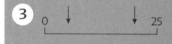

4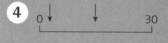

5

6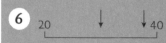

7 Estimate the number of digits in the number across the bottom of the page. Do not count them. Explain your method.

8 Estimate how many stacked pennies would reach 1 m high. Use your method to make the same estimation using stacks of other coins.

7 0 2 1 9 5 7 8 2 5 0 8 2 1 4 3 9 3 2 4 9 1 6 2 5 9 6 1 0 8 3 4 7 1 9 2 8 5 1 3 6 9 4 5 8 2

A

Example

Find a pair of numbers with a sum of 7 and a product of 12.
The answer is 3 and 4 because $3 + 4 = 7$ and $3 \times 4 = 12$.

Find a pair of numbers with:

1. a sum of 5 and a product of 6.

2. a sum of 9 and a product of 14.

3. a sum of 9 and a product of 20.

4. a sum of 12 and a product of 20.

5. a sum of 10 and a product of 25.

6. a sum of 9 and a product of 18.

7. a sum of 15 and a product of 50.

8. a sum of 8 and a product of 16.

B

Find the number.

1. below 50
   a multiple of 4
   the sum of its digits is 5

2. a 2-digit number
   a multiple of 7
   the product of its digits is 16

3. a square number
   below 50
   the sum of its digits is 9

4. a multiple of 3
   below 50
   the product of its digits is 20

5. a 2-digit number
   a multiple of 8
   the sum of its digits is 9

6. a square number
   a 2-digit number
   the product of its digits is 24

C

You may use a calculator.
Find 2 consecutive numbers with a product of:

1. 132
2. 210
3. 306
4. 156
5. 380
6. 240
7. 506
8. 420
9. 600
10. 702
11. 930
12. 812.

You may use a calculator.
Find 3 consecutive numbers with a total of:

13. 15
14. 27
15. 45
16. 60
17. 99
18. 333
19. 126
20. 303
21. 261
22. 111
23. 450
24. 237.

On this page you will learn:

> - **to round numbers to the nearest 10 or 100.**
> To round to the nearest 10 look at the units column.
> To round to the nearest 100 look at the tens column.
> If the number in that column is less than 5, round down.
> If the number in that column is 5 or greater than 5, round up.
>
> **Examples**
> $62 \rightarrow 60$ to nearest 10
> $165 \rightarrow 170$ to nearest 10
> $374 \rightarrow 400$ to nearest 100
>
> - **to approximate calculations by rounding.**
>
> **Examples** $38 + 23 \rightarrow 40 + 20 \rightarrow 60$ $29 \times 3 \rightarrow 30 \times 3 \rightarrow 90$

A

Round these numbers to the nearest 10.

1 21	**4** 83	**7** 78	**10** 92	**13** 55	**16** 87
2 35	**5** 69	**8** 42	**11** 64	**14** 34	**17** 96
3 47	**6** 51	**9** 26	**12** 16	**15** 73	**18** 22

B

Round to the nearest 10.

1 19	**2** 84	**3** 65	**4** 132	**5** 246	**6** 99

Round to the nearest 100.

7 230	**8** 650	**9** 370	**10** 420	**11** 910	**12** 880

Approximate by rounding to the nearest 10.

13 $62 + 57$	**15** $128 - 31$	**17** 39×2	**19** 18×5
14 $49 + 78$	**16** $92 - 49$	**18** 32×3	**20** 21×4

C

Round to the nearest

10	100	1000	Approximate by rounding to the nearest 10.	
1 713	**5** 841	**9** 4600	**13** $129 + 133$	**17** 29×6
2 247	**6** 9154	**10** 7150	**14** $608 + 199$	**18** 35×8
3 1492	**7** 4263	**11** 8520	**15** $552 - 347$	**19** 32×7
4 2635	**8** 1380	**12** 9370	**16** $743 - 126$	**20** 48×9

Copy the sentences, writing the numbers to the nearest 1000, with the word 'about'.

21 2813 patients were treated at the hospital.

22 The supermarket sold 1479 bottles of wine.

23 135 268 people live in the town.

24 There are 29 500 books in the library.

On this page you will learn to extend number sequences.

To find the rule that links the numbers study the gaps.

Examples

1   3   5   7   9   The rule is 'add 2'.
20   17   14   11   8   The rule is 'subtract 3'.

A

Write the first six numbers in each sequence.

	Start at	Rule			Start at	Rule
1	7	Add 2		7	34	Subtract 2
2	15	Add 5		8	97	Subtract 10
3	4	Add 4		9	22	Subtract 3
4	15	Add 3		10	26	Subtract 5
5	33	Add 10		11	36	Subtract 6
6	7	Add 7		12	30	Subtract 4

B

Copy and complete by filling in the boxes.

1 24 30 36 42 ☐ ☐
2 51 49 47 45 ☐ ☐
3 75 78 81 84 ☐ ☐
4 20 40 60 80 ☐ ☐
5 ☐ ☐ 44 39 34 29
6 ☐ ☐ 58 54 50 46

7 ☐ ☐ 38 45 52 59
8 ☐ ☐ 39 36 33 30
9 4 12 ☐ 28 ☐ 44
10 48 ☐ 36 ☐ 24 18
11 25 ☐ 75 100 125 ☐
12 ☐ 54 45 36 ☐ 18

C

Copy the sequences and write the next three numbers. What is the rule for each sequence?

1 57 59 61 63
2 126 122 118 114
3 46 53 60 67
4 65 56 47 38
5 30 70 110 150
6 137 134 131 128

7 35 60 85 110
8 28 36 44 52
9 78 73 68 63
10 12 27 42 57
11 475 450 425 400
12 57 63 69 75

13 105 90 75 60
14 93 86 79 72
15 7 15 23 31
16 243 354 465 576
17 19 22 25 28
18 141 130 119 108

On these pages you will learn to recognise and order negative numbers.

 Negative numbers
Below zero
Have a minus sign

 Positive numbers
Above zero

−10 −9 −8 −7 −6 −5 −4 −3 −2 −1 0 1 2 3 4 5 6 7 8 9 10

We often use negative numbers in the context of temperature.

Example

The temperature is 4°C. It falls 5°. What is the new temperature?
Answer −1°C

A

Use the number line above.

1. Count on 4 from −10.
2. Count on 3 from −5.
3. Count on 7 from −2.
4. Count on 5 from −5.

5. Count on 2 from −1.
6. Count on 4 from −3.
7. Count on 6 from −4.
8. Count on 8 from −2.

Copy and complete by filling in the boxes.

9. ☐ ☐ −3 −2 ☐ 0 1 2 ☐ 4 5

10. −10 −8 ☐ −4 −2 ☐ 2 ☐ ☐ 8 10

11. 5 4 ☐ ☐ 1 0 ☐ ☐ −3 −4 −5

12. 10 8 6 4 2 0 −2 ☐ ☐ ☐ ☐

Look at the scale.

13. What temperatures are shown by the letters?

14. Which letter shows the coldest temperature?

15. Give the difference in temperature between:
    a) A and B
    b) B and C
    c) A and C.

16. What would the temperature be if it was:
    a) at B and rose 3°C?
    b) at B and rose 5°C?

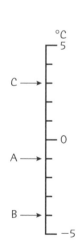

B

Use the number line on the opposite page.

1. Count on 6 from −5.
2. Count on 8 from −10.
3. Count on 10 from −6.
4. Count on 6 from −4.

5. Count back 8 from 5.
6. Count back 7 from 0.
7. Count back 15 from 8.
8. Count back 13 from 4.

Copy and complete by filling in the boxes.

9. 3 2 ☐ ☐ ☐ −2 −3
10. ☐ ☐ ☐ 1 2 3 4
11. ☐ ☐ −4 −6 −8 −10 ☐
12. −10 ☐ −8 ☐ −6 ☐ −4

13. −10 −8 ☐ −4 ☐ ☐ 2
14. −7 ☐ ☐ −1 1 3 5
15. 6 4 2 ☐ ☐ ☐ −6
16. 5 ☐ 1 ☐ −3 ☐ −7

17. What temperatures are shown by the letters?
18. Which letter shows the coldest temperature?
19. Give the difference in temperature between
    a) A and B
    b) A and C
    c) B and C.
20. What would the temperature be if it was:
    a) at A and fell 7°?
    b) at B and rose 9°?

C

Find the difference between each pair of numbers.

1. −6 −4
2. −2 2
3. −3 5
4. −1 3
5. −4 2
6. −1 −7
7. 0 −4
8. 2 −3

Put these numbers in order, smallest first.

9.
−3	0	−1
2	5	

10.
4	−3	
−1	−5	1

11.
3	0	−4
−2	1	

12.
2	−4	
4	−1	0

Copy and complete these tables showing changes in temperature.

13.
Monday	Change	Tuesday
3°C	−4°C	−1°C
−1°C	+3°C	
0°C	−5°C	
4°C	−7°C	
−6°C	+2°C	
−2°C	+4°C	

14.
Monday	Change	Tuesday
7°C	−4°C	3°C
−2°C		3°C
−4°C		−1°C
1°C		−3°C
0°C		−6°C
−3°C		4°C

On this page you will learn to recognise odd and even numbers and to give examples that match general statements about odd or even numbers.

An even number is a number which can be divided exactly by 2.
An odd number cannot be divided by 2 without leaving a remainder.

Examples $14 \div 2 = 7$ 14 is even.

$15 \div 2 = 7$ remainder 1 15 is odd.

A

3	6	7	18	24	31
49	52	65	78	83	94

1 Which of the above numbers is odd?

2 Which of the above numbers is even?

3 If you add two even numbers is the answer odd or even?
Is this always true? Give three examples.

B

1 Give the next odd number after each number in the box.

2 Give the next even number after each number in the box.

102	216	727	338
949	255	863	174
581	690	205	411

3 If you add two odd numbers is the answer odd or even?
Is this always true? Give four examples.

C

Use each set of numbers. Make six 3-digit numbers.
How many of your numbers are odd? How many are even?

1 3, 1, 2 **2** 5, 9, 7 **3** 2, 4, 8 **4** 5, 4, 6

Copy and complete these rules by writing odd or even in the box.

5 When you add an odd number and an even number the answer is always ☐.

6 The difference between two even numbers is always ☐.

7 The difference between two odd numbers is always ☐.

8 The difference between an odd number and an even number is always ☐.

9 Give four examples for each rule.

MULTIPLES

On this page you will learn to recognise multiples.

Multiples are the numbers in a multiplication table.
Examples
The multiples of 2 are the numbers in the 2 times table.
2, 4, 6, 8, 10, 12 . . . 28, 30, 32, 34 . . . 116, 118, 120, and so on.

10, 20, 30, 80, 500, 730 and 1000 are all multiples of 10.

A number may be a multiple of more than one number.
Examples
16 is a multiple of 1, 2, 4, 8 and 16.   14 is a multiple of 1, 2, 7 and 14.

A

Write down the first five multiples of:

1 2   **4** 3
2 5   **5** 4
3 10   **6** 6.

7 Is 26 a multiple of 2?
8 Is 27 a multiple of 3?
9 Is 75 a multiple of 7?
10 Is 34 a multiple of 6?

11 Is 54 a multiple of 5?
12 Is 32 a multiple of 4?
13 Is 80 a multiple of 8?
14 Is 35 a multiple of 5?

15 Is 23 a multiple of 3?
16 Is 24 a multiple of 6?
17 Is 70 a multiple of 10?
18 Is 25 a multiple of 2?

19 Is 18 a multiple of 3?
20 Is 14 a multiple of 4?
21 Is 29 a multiple of 9?
22 Is 40 a multiple of 5?

B

Which number should not be in the box?

1 Multiples of 2
6, 41, 74, 100

2 Multiples of 4
16, 28, 34, 24

3 Multiples of 10
5, 30, 110, 70

4 Multiples of 8
88, 32, 72, 58

Which of the numbers in the ring are multiples of:
5 2   **7** 5
6 3   **8** 6?

9, 14, 15, 18, 25, 27, 30

Find a number that is a multiple of both:
9 3 and 4   **11** 2 and 3
10 5 and 10   **12** 3 and 5.

C

Which of the numbers in the box are multiples of:
1 2   **3** 6
2 5   **4** 9?

| 12 | 15 | 17 | 18 | 20 |
| 24 | 25 | 36 | 42 | 60 |

Find two numbers that are multiples of both:
5 4 and 10   **7** 4 and 9
6 3 and 7   **8** 5 and 6.

Use these digits.

Make as many 2-digit numbers as you can that are multiples of:
9 2   **11** 4
10 5   **12** 3.

13 Write down the 6th multiple of:
a) 8   d) 20
b) 11   e) 9
c) 7   f) 15.

On these pages you will learn to read and write fractions correctly.

A fraction is a number that is less than a whole one.
When a whole one is divided into <u>equal</u> parts each of the parts is a fraction of the whole one.

Example

3 equal parts $\frac{1}{3}$ is shaded.

$\frac{2}{3}$ is unshaded.

Here are some words that you will need.

$\frac{1}{2}$ one half $\frac{1}{3}$ one third $\frac{1}{4}$ one quarter $\frac{1}{5}$ one fifth

$\frac{1}{6}$ one sixth $\frac{1}{8}$ one eighth $\frac{1}{10}$ one tenth $\frac{1}{12}$ one twelfth

What fraction of each diagram is shaded?
Write your answers in figures and in words.

1   **4**   **7**   **10**

2   **5**    **8**   **11**

3   **6**   **9**   **12**

13 Draw a grid like the one shown.

Shade in $\frac{7}{16}$ of the squares.

Put × in $\frac{1}{4}$ of the squares.

B

What fraction of each diagram is shaded?
Write your answers in figures and in words.

C

What fraction of each diagram is:
a) shaded?   b) unshaded?
Write your answers in figures and in words.

13 Draw a grid like the one shown.

Shade in $\frac{2}{3}$ of the squares.

Put × in $\frac{5}{8}$ of the squares.

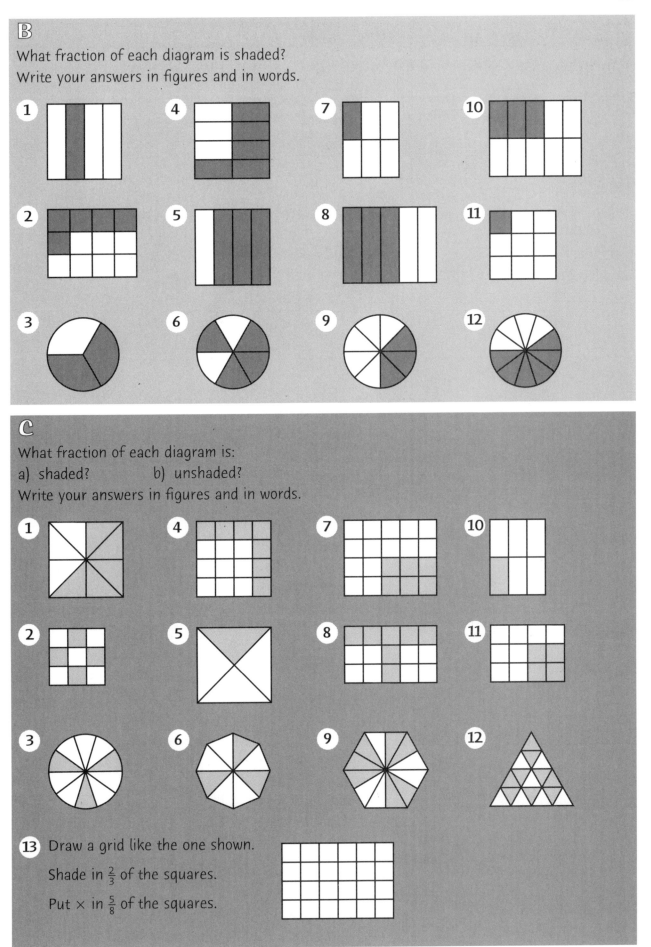

On these pages you will learn to recognise equivalent fractions.

Equivalent fractions are fractions that look different but are the same.

Examples

 $\dfrac{1}{2} = \dfrac{2}{4}$

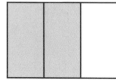 $\dfrac{2}{3} = \dfrac{4}{6}$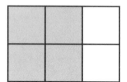

A

Write the equivalent fractions shown by the shaded areas in each pair of diagrams.

1

2

3

4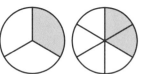

5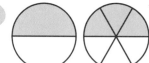

6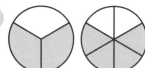

7

8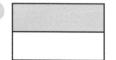

9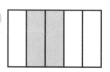

10

11

12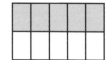

13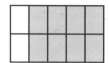

14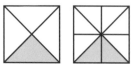

15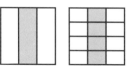

16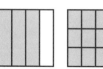

B

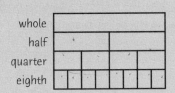

Use the fraction charts. Copy and complete these equivalent fractions by filling in the box.

1 $1 = \dfrac{\square}{3}$

2 $\dfrac{1}{2} = \dfrac{\square}{4}$

3 $\dfrac{2}{5} = \dfrac{\square}{10}$

4 $\dfrac{1}{2} = \dfrac{\square}{6}$

5 $\dfrac{1}{5} = \dfrac{\square}{10}$

6 $1 = \dfrac{\square}{6}$

7 $\dfrac{1}{2} = \dfrac{\square}{8}$

8 $1 = \dfrac{\square}{10}$

9 $\dfrac{1}{4} = \dfrac{\square}{8}$

10 $\dfrac{1}{2} = \dfrac{\square}{10}$

11 $1 = \dfrac{\square}{8}$

12 $\dfrac{1}{3} = \dfrac{\square}{6}$

Copy and complete these fraction chains.

13 $\dfrac{1}{2} = \dfrac{\square}{4} = \dfrac{\square}{6} = \dfrac{\square}{8} = \dfrac{\square}{10} = \dfrac{\square}{12} = \dfrac{\square}{14} = \dfrac{\square}{16} = \dfrac{\square}{18} = \dfrac{\square}{20}$

14 $\dfrac{1}{3} = \dfrac{2}{\square} = \dfrac{3}{\square} = \dfrac{4}{\square} = \dfrac{5}{\square} = \dfrac{6}{\square} = \dfrac{7}{\square} = \dfrac{8}{\square} = \dfrac{9}{\square} = \dfrac{10}{\square}$

15 $\dfrac{3}{4} = \dfrac{\square}{\square} = \dfrac{9}{12} = \dfrac{\square}{16} = \dfrac{15}{\square} = \dfrac{\square}{\square} = \dfrac{\square}{\square} = \dfrac{\square}{\square} = \dfrac{\square}{\square} = \dfrac{\square}{\square}$

C

Copy and complete by writing the missing sign: >, < or =.

1 $\dfrac{1}{2} \;\square\; \dfrac{3}{8}$

2 $\dfrac{1}{3} \;\square\; \dfrac{2}{6}$

3 $\dfrac{2}{5} \;\square\; \dfrac{5}{10}$

4 $\dfrac{3}{4} \;\square\; \dfrac{5}{10}$

5 $\dfrac{5}{6} \;\square\; \dfrac{10}{12}$

6 $\dfrac{3}{5} \;\square\; \dfrac{11}{20}$

7 $\dfrac{7}{8} \;\square\; \dfrac{14}{16}$

8 $\dfrac{2}{3} \;\square\; \dfrac{9}{12}$

9 $\dfrac{1}{2} \;\square\; \dfrac{9}{20}$

10 $\dfrac{3}{4} \;\square\; \dfrac{12}{16}$

11 $\dfrac{1}{3} \;\square\; \dfrac{6}{12}$

12 $\dfrac{7}{10} \;\square\; \dfrac{13}{20}$

Which is the odd one out in these sets of fractions?

13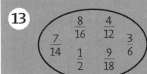

14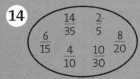

15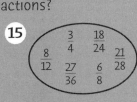

16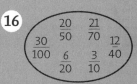

17 Match the fractions to the letters on the number line from 0 to 1.

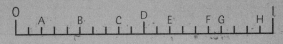

$\dfrac{1}{4}$ $\dfrac{8}{10}$ $\dfrac{3}{5}$ $\dfrac{2}{20}$ $\dfrac{1}{2}$ $\dfrac{95}{100}$ $\dfrac{3}{4}$ $\dfrac{20}{50}$

On this page you will learn to find a fraction of a number or quantity.

Examples

$\frac{1}{5}$ of 30 = 30 ÷ 5 = 6
       = 6

$\frac{3}{10}$ of 40 = (40 ÷ 10) × 3.
       = 4 × 3
       = 12

What fraction of £1 is 5p?
Twenty 5p's make £1.
5p is $\frac{1}{20}$ of £1.

A

Find $\frac{1}{2}$ of:

1. 12
2. 24
3. 18p
4. 40p
5. 100 cm

6. 16
7. 30
8. 60p
9. 28p
10. 50 cm.

Find $\frac{1}{10}$ of:

11. 30
12. 40
13. 90p
14. 50p
15. 80 cm

16. 20
17. 10
18. 70p
19. 100p
20. 60 cm.

Find $\frac{1}{5}$ of:

21. 20
22. 100
23. 15p
24. 30p
25. 25 cm

26. 50
27. 40
28. 35p
29. 10p
30. 45 cm.

31. There are 34 ducks on a pond. One half of them are green. How many green ducks are there?

B

Find

1. $\frac{1}{2}$ of 22
2. $\frac{1}{5}$ of 25
3. $\frac{1}{10}$ of 80
4. $\frac{1}{4}$ of 24
5. $\frac{1}{3}$ of 15 cm
6. $\frac{1}{2}$ of 1 m
7. $\frac{1}{5}$ of £1.00
8. $\frac{1}{10}$ of £1.00
9. $\frac{1}{4}$ of 80p
10. $\frac{1}{3}$ of 24p.

What fraction of:

11. £1 is 10p?
12. £1 is 50p?
13. £1 is 20p?
14. £1 is 25p?
15. 1 m is 1 cm?
16. 1 m is 25 cm?
17. 1 m is 10 cm?
18. 1 m is 50 cm?

19. 60 ice creams are sold. One third of the ice creams are vanilla flavour and one quarter are chocolate flavour.
    a) How many vanilla ice creams are sold?
    b) How many chocolate ice creams are sold?

C

Find

1. $\frac{3}{4}$ of 28
2. $\frac{4}{5}$ of 30
3. $\frac{2}{3}$ of 18
4. $\frac{7}{10}$ of 20
5. $\frac{3}{10}$ of 500
6. $\frac{1}{100}$ of 700
7. $\frac{9}{10}$ of 1 m
8. $\frac{32}{100}$ of 1 m
9. $\frac{6}{10}$ of 50p
10. $\frac{51}{100}$ of £1.00.

What fraction of:

11. £2 is 50p?
12. £2 is 10p?
13. £5 is 50p?
14. £5 is 10p?
15. 2 m is 50 cm?
16. 2 m is 10 cm?
17. 4 m is 50 cm?
18. 4 m is 10 cm?

19. There are 28 children in a class. Five sevenths of the children do not use a pen. How many of the children do use a pen?

20. There are 12 eggs in a box. Two thirds of them are broken. How many eggs are unbroken?

On this page you will solve simple problems involving ratio and proportion.

A

1 In a Lucky Dip 1 ticket in every 5 wins a prize.
Copy and complete the table.

Number of tickets	5									
Number of prizes	1	2	3	4	5	6	7	8	9	10

2 Make a similar table for a Lucky Dip in which 1 ticket in every 4 wins a prize.

B

Copy and complete these sentences for each of the patterns below.
Write both sentences for each pattern.

1 **2** **3**

a) 1 in every ☐ squares is shaded.

b) There are ☐ white squares to every 1 shaded square.

Draw a tile pattern like those above in which:

4 1 in every 5 squares is shaded.

5 There are 3 white squares to every shaded square.

6 1 in every 3 squares is shaded.

C

1 At the Chess Club there is one girl for every three boys.
There are 4 girls at the club. How many boys are there?

2 Kylie has four times as many sweets as Jade.
Jade has 8 sweets. How many sweets does Kylie have?

3 Two in every three people watching a film are children.
There are 150 people in the cinema. How many are adults?

4 Josh has read half as many pages of his book as Brandon. Brandon has read 62 pages.
How many pages has Josh read?

5 There are five red marbles for every 2 green marbles in a jar.
There are 25 red marbles in the jar. How many green marbles are there?

6 Three in every seven ice creams sold are vanilla flavour. 21 vanilla ice creams are sold.
How many ice creams are sold altogether?

On these pages you will learn:

- **to know what decimal fractions are.**

Decimals are a way of expressing fractions. The decimal point separates the whole number from the fractions.

Examples

$2\frac{3}{10} = 2 \cdot 3$

$1\frac{53}{100} = 1 \cdot 53$

- **You will also learn the value of the digits in a decimal fraction.**

The value of a digit depends upon its position in a number.

Each digit in a number is 10 times higher than the digit to the right. This applies to decimal fractions as well as to whole numbers.

Examples

$$T \ U \cdot \tfrac{1}{10} \ \tfrac{1}{100}$$
$$30 = 3 \ 0 \cdot 0$$
$$3 = \ \ 3 \cdot 0$$
$$\tfrac{3}{10} = \ \ 0 \cdot 3$$
$$\tfrac{3}{100} = \ \ 0 \cdot 0 \ 3$$

$$H \ T \ U \cdot \tfrac{1}{10} \ \tfrac{1}{100}$$
$$700 = 7 \ 0 \ 0 \cdot 0$$
$$70 = \ \ 7 \ 0 \cdot 0$$
$$7 = \ \ \ \ 7 \cdot 0$$
$$\tfrac{7}{10} = \ \ \ \ 0 \cdot 7$$
$$\tfrac{7}{100} = \ \ \ \ 0 \cdot 0 \ 7$$

A

What part of each shape is shaded? Write your answer as a fraction and as a decimal fraction.

Write the numbers shown by each of the arrows on the 0 to 1 number line as:
a) a fraction.
b) a decimal fraction.

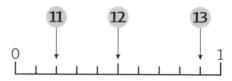

B

Write each number shown by the arrows as a decimal fraction.

Give the value of the underlined figure in each of these numbers.

7   6.<u>8</u>   11   <u>1</u>8.2   15   <u>1</u>9.32
8   1<u>4</u>.9   12   24.<u>1</u>   16   12.<u>4</u>6
9   0.<u>7</u>   13   <u>3</u>.07   17   0.<u>5</u>2
10 <u>5</u>.3   14   8.<u>6</u>4   18   106.<u>8</u>

Give the next five terms in each of these sequences.

19   0.1   0.2   0.3   0.4   0.5
20   0.2   0.4   0.6   0.8   1.0
21   0.5   1.0   1.5   2.0   2.5
22   0.1   0.3   0.5   0.7   0.9

Copy and complete by filling in the box.

23   0.6 + 0.1 = ☐   29   1.4 + 0.4 = ☐
24   0.3 + 0.2 = ☐   30   1.2 + 0.5 = ☐
25   0.5 + 0.3 = ☐   31   1.1 + 0.8 = ☐
26   0.7 − 0.3 = ☐   32   1.9 − 0.5 = ☐
27   0.9 − 0.6 = ☐   33   1.6 − 0.4 = ☐
28   0.8 − 0.2 = ☐   34   1.7 − 0.3 = ☐

Copy and complete.

35   0.5 − ☐ = 0.3   41   1.3 + ☐ = 1.9
36   0.4 + ☐ = 0.9   42   1.8 − ☐ = 1.6
37   0.8 − ☐ = 0.4   43   1.1 + ☐ = 1.8
38   ☐ + 0.1 = 0.7   44   ☐ − 0.3 = 1.2
39   ☐ − 0.3 = 0.6   45   ☐ + 0.4 = 1.6
40   ☐ + 0.5 = 0.7   46   ☐ − 0.2 = 1.7

C

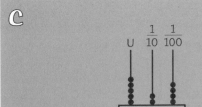

Example

5 units   2 tenths   4 hundredths
The number shown is 5.24.

Write the decimal fraction shown on each abacus.

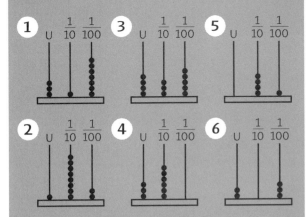

Give the value of the underlined figure in each of these numbers.

7   0.<u>9</u>   13   2.<u>9</u>6   19   16.<u>2</u>3
8   <u>1</u>0.4   14   <u>3</u>5.42   20   25.0<u>4</u>
9   <u>2</u>4.7   15   41.<u>7</u>8   21   <u>5</u>.13
10 18.<u>7</u>6   16   <u>1</u>7.49   22   78.0<u>6</u>
11 13.<u>9</u>1   17   7.<u>3</u>4   23   100.8<u>3</u>
12 2<u>6</u>.58   18   32.5<u>7</u>   24   136.<u>5</u>9

Write the answer only.

25   1.5 + 0.4   33   0.2 + 0.8
26   2.3 + 0.7   34   0.6 + 1.1
27   1.3 − 0.3   35   1.8 − 1.4
28   1.6 − 0.7   36   2.1 − 0.8
29   3.8 + 0.5   37   1.8 + 1.6
30   1.5 + 1.9   38   2.3 + 0.9
31   2.4 − 0.6   39   3.2 − 0.8
32   1.7 − 0.9   40   4.5 − 0.6

On this page you will learn to order a set of decimals.

Write the set of decimals in a line with the decimal points in a column.
Fill in any empty spaces with zeros. This makes it easier to compare the decimals.

Example

Arrange 1·4, 0·41, 2 and 1·2 in order.

Write in column.	Put in zeros.	Arrange in order.
1·4	1·40	0·41
0·41	0·41	1·2
2	2·00	1·4
1·2	1·20	2

A

Write the larger of these pairs of numbers.

1 16   1·6 **3** 0·8   8·0 **5** 1·9   0·9 **7** 3·2   2·3 **9** 4   1·4

2 1·2   2·0 **4** 5   0·5 **6** 1·8   8 **8** 0·7   6·7 **10** 6·3   3·6

11 Copy the line. Put each number from the box on the number line.

0·2   0·5   0·9   0·4   0·7

0   1

B

Copy and complete by writing >, < or = in the box.

1 0·6 ☐ 6·0   **3** 0·5 ☐ 0·50   **5** 46 ☐ 6·4   **7** 8·0 ☐ 8

2 14 ☐ 1·4   **4** 2·7 ☐ 7·2   **6** 1·1 ☐ 11   **8** 38 ☐ 8·3

Arrange the decimals in order. Start with the smallest.

9 4·7   7·4   3·6   6·3   **11** 21   2·1   1·2   12   **13** 8·4   48   8   4·8

10 9·2   2·2   2·9   9·9   **12** 5·3   5   3   3·5   **14** 7·9   7   7·7   9·7

C

Arrange the decimals in order.
Start with the smallest.

1 3·4   33·4   4·3   43·3   43

2 11·9   9·1   9·01   19·1   1·9

3 14·1   1·4   1·41   11·4   4·1

4 7·73   8·7   7·83   8·37   8·73

5 9·6   5·69   9·65   9·5   5·96

6 Copy the line. Put each number from the box on the number line.

0·97   1·08   0·91   1·0   1·05   0·94

0·9   1.1

On this page you will learn to recognise equivalent fractions and decimals.

It is important to remember that:

$\frac{1}{10} = 0.1$ $\frac{2}{10} = 0.2$ $\frac{3}{10} = 0.3$ $\frac{1}{2} = 0.5$ $\frac{1}{4} = 0.25$ $\frac{3}{4} = 0.75$ and so on

A

Copy and complete by writing a decimal in the box.

1 $\frac{1}{10} = \square$ **4** $\frac{3}{10} = \square$

2 $\frac{1}{4} = \square$ **5** $\frac{3}{4} = \square$

3 $\frac{1}{2} = \square$ **6** $\frac{6}{10} = \square$

Write the larger amount of money from each pair.

7 12p £0.20

8 77p £0.70

9 41p £0.40

10 £0.13 8p

11 £0.90 99p

12 £0.07 50p

13 Match each fraction with one of the decimals.

$\frac{1}{2}$	0.25
$\frac{1}{10}$	0.4
$\frac{7}{10}$	0.1
$\frac{3}{4}$	0.5
$\frac{1}{4}$	0.7
$\frac{4}{10}$	0.75

B

Write as fractions.

1 0.4   **3** 0.1   **5** 0.25

2 0.5   **4** 0.6   **6** 0.3

Write as decimals.

7 £$\frac{7}{10}$ **10** $\frac{1}{2}$ cm

8 £$\frac{1}{10}$ **11** $\frac{8}{10}$ m

9 £$\frac{3}{4}$ **12** $\frac{2}{10}$ m

Copy and complete by writing >, < or = in the box.

13 $\frac{1}{2} \square 0.2$

14 $\frac{1}{4} \square 0.4$

15 $\frac{3}{4} \square 0.3$

16 $\frac{9}{10} \square 0.9$

17 Copy and complete the table.

Decimals	Fractions
	$\frac{3}{10}$
	$\frac{9}{10}$
	$\frac{1}{2}$
	$\frac{10}{10}$
	$\frac{1}{4}$
0.2	
0.7	
0.75	
0.1	

C

Write as whole numbers and fractions.
(Example $3.25 = 3\frac{1}{4}$)

1 1.5   **7** 5.25

2 3.8   **8** 17.43

3 7.3   **9** 6.82

4 2.7   **10** 8.75

5 4.9   **11** 13.14

6 11.6   **12** 20.09

Write as decimals.

13 $1\frac{1}{2}$ **19** £$6\frac{9}{10}$

14 $3\frac{7}{10}$ **20** £$3\frac{1}{2}$

15 $4\frac{1}{4}$ **21** £$\frac{72}{100}$

16 $9\frac{4}{10}$ **22** $1\frac{3}{4}$ m

17 $2\frac{8}{10}$ **23** $5\frac{3}{10}$ cm

18 $2\frac{3}{4}$ **24** $\frac{73}{100}$ m

Write in ascending order.

25 $\frac{1}{2}$, 0.2, 0.12

26 0.34, $\frac{3}{4}$, $\frac{3}{10}$

27 0.7, 0.17, $\frac{7}{100}$

28 $\frac{4}{10}$, 0.44, $\frac{1}{4}$

Give the answer as a decimal.

29 $\frac{1}{4} + 0.3$

30 $\frac{1}{2} - 0.2$

31 $0.46 + \frac{7}{100}$

32 $0.87 - \frac{1}{10}$

33 $\frac{3}{4} - 0.13$

34 $0.29 + \frac{1}{10}$

On these pages you will learn:

- **to understand the operation of addition.**

  The order in which you add numbers does not change the answer.

Example A

$74 + 37 = 37 + 74 = 111$

Example B

$38 + 27 + 19 = (38 + 27) + 19 = 65 + 19 = 84$
$38 + 27 + 19 = 38 + (27 + 19) = 38 + 46 = 84$

- **addition is the inverse of subtraction.**

Example

Find the missing number. $\square + 24 = 39$

The missing number is 15 because
$39 - 24 = 15$.

- **to understand the vocabulary of addition.**

Example

$53 + 18$ can be expressed in different ways.

the sum of 53 and 18
the total of 53 and 18
53 and 18 altogether
53 increased by 18
53 add 18
18 greater than 53
18 more than 53
53 plus 18

A

Work out

1 The sum of 65 and 35.
2 37 add 15.
3 The total of 80 and 23.

4 10 greater than 94.
5 36 and 23 altogether.
6 19 more than 28.

7 700 increased by 300.
8 14 plus 14.
9 Add 84 to 500.

10 The sum of 54 and 25.
11 The total of 900 and 500.
12 Increase 66 by 21.

Write True or False for each of these number sentences.

13 $8 + 16 = 16 + 8$
14 $35 + 9 = 9 + 35$
15 $24 + 7 = 42 + 7$

16 $13 + 12 = 12 + 13$
17 $41 + 16 = 14 + 61$
18 $3 + 4 + 5 = 5 + 4 + 3$

19 $17 + 19 = 19 + 19$
20 $7 + 8 + 9 = 6 + 7 + 8$
21 $5 + 6 + 7 = 6 + 7 + 5$

22 Find all the different totals you can make using three of these four numbers.

B

Copy and complete by writing the missing number in the box.

1 The total of 150 and 34 is ☐.

2 The total of 47 and ☐ is 100.

3 ☐ add 51 is 117.

4 39 greater than 128 is ☐.

5 262 and ☐ is 300 altogether.

6 ☐ is 30 more than 155.

7 164 increased by 7 is ☐.

8 173 plus ☐ is 200.

9 ☐ added to 2300 is 3000.

10 The total of 120 and 52 is ☐.

11 The sum of ☐ and 46 is 83.

12 ☐ increased by 84 is 122.

Find the totals. Work downwards first. Check your answers by working upwards. Which way was easier?

13
```
  17
  18
+ 32
```

15
```
  35
  16
+ 12
```

17
```
  15
  25
+ 18
```

14
```
  12
  18
+ 45
```

16
```
  19
  17
+ 13
```

18
```
  28
  11
+ 19
```

Copy and complete by writing the missing number in the box.

19 $700 + ☐ = 1100$

20 $☐ + 20 = 67$

21 $☐ + 31 = 69$

22 $474 + ☐ = 500$

23 $☐ + 38 = 64$

24 $☐ + 36 = 356$

25 $63 + ☐ = 100$

26 $☐ + 19 = 85$

C

Find the totals, working from left to right. Check your answers by working from right to left.

1 $48 + 32 + 27$

2 $42 + 37 + 63$

3 $77 + 65 + 55$

4 $49 + 21 + 28$

5 $27 + 62 + 38$

6 $36 + 54 + 48$

7 $63 + 27 + 49$

8 $37 + 46 + 34$

9 $35 + 45 + 76$

10 $45 + 39 + 51$

11 $68 + 52 + 37$

12 $57 + 47 + 43$

Copy and complete by writing the missing number in the box.

13 $800 + ☐ = 1700$

14 $☐ + 741 = 1241$

15 $☐ + 0.7 = 7$

16 $230 + ☐ = 510$

17 $☐ + 61 = 136$

18 $☐ + 180 = 820$

19 $359 + ☐ = 789$

20 $☐ + 120 = 532$

21 $☐ + 49 = 218$

22 $0.4 + ☐ = 1$

23 Write $136 + 94$ in words in eight different ways.

24 Find all the different totals you can make using three of these five numbers.

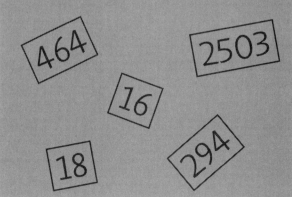

On these pages you will learn to understand the vocabulary and operation of subtraction.

TAKING AWAY

Examples

1. 9 take away 5.
2. 9 subtract 5.
3. Take away 5 from 9.
4. Subtract 5 from 9.

FINDING A DIFFERENCE

Examples

1. What is the difference between 12 and 5?
2. How many more is 12 than 5?
3. How many less is 5 than 12?

THE INVERSE OF ADDITION

Examples

1. Find the missing number.

   $\square - 19 = 46$

   The answer is 65 because $46 + 19 = 65$.

2. How many must be added to 37 to make 93?

   The answer is 56 because $93 - 37 = 56$.

A

Work out

1. 35 less than 100.
2. Take 196 from 204.
3. 57 subtract 31.

4. 300 take away 9.
5. 26 less than 78.
6. Subtract 400 from 1000.

Copy and complete by writing the missing number in the box.

7. $120 - \square = 90$
8. $238 - \square = 231$
9. $\square - 9 = 264$
10. $\square - 35 = 24$
11. $134 - \square = 94$
12. $814 - \square = 714$
13. $\square - 41 = 27$
14. $\square - 10 = 694$
15. $500 - \square = 492$
16. $1200 - \square = 700$
17. $\square - 29 = 67$
18. $\square - 11 = 124$

Find the difference between these numbers and:

⑨   ⑪

19. 133
20. 76
21. 251
22. 348
23. 125
24. 93

How many more must be added to these numbers to make the target number?

⑩⓪   ⑩⓪⓪

25. 75
26. 97
27. 15
28. 300
29. 500
30. 200

B

1. 322 subtract 60.
2. Take 35 from 67.
3. 26 less than 82.

4. Subtract 19 from 83.
5. 98 less than 206.
6. 100 take away 28.

Copy and complete by writing the missing number in the box.

7. $74 - \square = 36$
8. $503 - \square = 8$
9. $\square - 400 = 800$

13. $\square - 850 = 150$
14. $\square - 21 = 255$
15. $3000 - \square = 4$

10. $\square - 29 = 35$
11. $600 - \square = 58$
12. $135 - \square = 87$

16. $100 - \square = 47$
17. $\square - 60 = 70$
18. $\square - 50 = 167$

Find the difference between these numbers and:

  (31)   (19)

19. 164
20. 257
21. 83

22. 336
23. 198
24. 145

How many more must be added to these numbers to make:

 (100)   (1000)

25. 38
26. 74
27. 41

28. 350
29. 50
30. 550

How many less is each of these numbers than:

(76)   (168)

31. 34
32. 19
33. 51

34. 57
35. 99
36. 115

C

Find the difference between each pair of numbers.

1. 52   217
2. 4003   1998
3. 620   280
4. 39   485

5. 1572   800
6. 320   634
7. 503   294
8. 324   62

9. Write $87 - 54$ in as many ways as you can.

10. Copy and complete the table showing children's marks in an end of year English Test.

Name	Paper A	Paper B	Total
Total	80	80	160
Emily	77		152
Oliver	74		146
Nathan	71		140
Kerry	68		125
Tracey	62		121
Anil		59	117
Ben		50	113
Rachel		46	111
Craig		45	104
Jeremy		39	88
Charlene		37	83

11. Find the six differences that you can make using pairs of these four numbers.

68   200   175   312

12. A motorist is driving 250 miles. She stops for petrol after 89 miles. How much further does she have to go?

On this page you will practise using addition facts.

A

Work out

1 8 + 6
2 7 + 7
3 5 + 8
4 7 + 9
5 9 + 8

6 6 + 7
7 9 + 6
8 9 + 9
9 6 + 8
10 8 + 7

11 8 + 8
12 8 + 9
13 7 + 6
14 9 + 7
15 7 + 8

Take one number from each box. Find all six number sentences.

16
| 85 | | 55 |
| 15 | + | 15 | = 100
45		65
35		5
95		25
75		85

17
| 400 | | 100 |
| 900 | + | 200 | = 1000
800		300
700		700
500		600
300		500

B

Work out

1 60 + 80
2 90 + 70
3 80 + 80
4 50 + 90
5 90 + 60

6 70 + 80
7 700 + 700
8 900 + 900
9 800 + 900
10 700 + 800

11 50 + 90
12 80 + 80
13 600 + 700
14 900 + 400
15 700 + 900

Take one number from each box. Find all six number sentences.

16
| 47 | | 45 |
| 14 | | 61 |
| 39 | + | 9 | = 100
91		27
55		53
73		86

17
| 350 | | 350 |
| 450 | | 850 |
| 150 | + | 750 | = 1000
250		950
650		550
50		650

C

Copy and complete.

1 60 + ☐ = 170
2 ☐ + 90 = 140
3 70 + ☐ = 140
4 ☐ + 800 = 1400
5 700 + ☐ = 1600

6 ☐ + 600 = 1300
7 0·9 + ☐ = 1·8
8 ☐ + 0·7 = 1·5
9 0·8 + ☐ = 1·6
10 ☐ + 0·9 = 1·7

What needs to be added to each number in the outer ring to make the target number?
Example 490 + 510 = 1000

11 a)

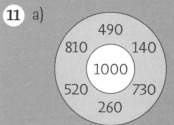

b)

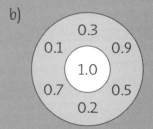

12 Find five pairs of three-digit numbers that total 1000. You cannot use 0.

On this page you will practise using subtraction facts.

A

Work out

1. $15 - 7$
2. $17 - 8$
3. $14 - 6$
4. $13 - 7$
5. $16 - 9$

6. $15 - 8$
7. $18 - 9$
8. $13 - 5$
9. $16 - 8$
10. $16 - 7$

11. $17 - 9$
12. $14 - 7$
13. $13 - 6$
14. $15 - 9$
15. $15 - 6$

Take one number from each box. Find all six number sentences.

16.
$$100 - \begin{array}{|c|} \hline 95 \\ 25 \\ 65 \\ 55 \\ 75 \\ 5 \\ \hline \end{array} = \begin{array}{|c|} \hline 95 \\ 5 \\ 25 \\ 75 \\ 35 \\ 45 \\ \hline \end{array}$$

17.
$$1000 - \begin{array}{|c|} \hline 700 \\ 600 \\ 100 \\ 200 \\ 400 \\ 900 \\ \hline \end{array} = \begin{array}{|c|} \hline 600 \\ 100 \\ 400 \\ 900 \\ 300 \\ 800 \\ \hline \end{array}$$

B

Work out

1. $140 - 70$
2. $150 - 80$
3. $180 - 90$
4. $170 - 80$
5. $150 - 60$

6. $140 - 50$
7. $1500 - 700$
8. $1600 - 800$
9. $1600 - 900$
10. $1400 - 600$

11. $150 - 90$
12. $1300 - 600$
13. $1700 - 900$
14. $160 - 70$
15. $1400 - 800$

Take one number from each box. Find all six number sentences.

16.
$$100 - \begin{array}{|c|} \hline 52 \\ 23 \\ 46 \\ 81 \\ 18 \\ 67 \\ \hline \end{array} = \begin{array}{|c|} \hline 77 \\ 33 \\ 48 \\ 54 \\ 19 \\ 82 \\ \hline \end{array}$$

17.
$$1000 - \begin{array}{|c|} \hline 550 \\ 150 \\ 250 \\ 50 \\ 450 \\ 850 \\ \hline \end{array} = \begin{array}{|c|} \hline 150 \\ 450 \\ 950 \\ 850 \\ 750 \\ 550 \\ \hline \end{array}$$

C

Copy and complete.

1. $160 - \square = 80$
2. $150 - \square = 70$
3. $170 - \square = 90$
4. $1500 - \square = 600$
5. $1800 - \square = 900$

6. $1400 - \square = 700$
7. $1 \cdot 5 - \square = 0 \cdot 8$
8. $1 \cdot 6 - \square = 0 \cdot 9$
9. $1 \cdot 7 - \square = 0 \cdot 8$
10. $\square + 0 \cdot 9 = 1 \cdot 7$

Find the difference between each number in the outer ring and the target number.
Example $1000 - 690 = 310$

11. a)

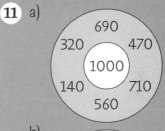

b)

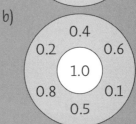

Copy and complete.

12. $140 - \square = 200 - 80$
13. $1200 - 400 = \square - 700$
14. $\square - 76 = 100 - 20$
15. $1 \cdot 5 - 0 \cdot 8 = 1 \cdot 0 - \square$

On this page you will learn to find a difference by counting up through the next multiple of 10, 100 or 1000.

Examples $94 - 47 = 3 + 40 + 4$ $403 - 386 = 4 + 10 + 3$ $4003 - 3985 = 5 + 10 + 3$

$= 47$ $= 17$ $= 18$

A
Work out
1. $32 - 26$
2. $51 - 47$
3. $64 - 55$
4. $85 - 78$
5. $40 - 22$
6. $50 - 27$
7. $100 - 86$
8. $200 - 192$
9. $400 - 381$
10. $103 - 90$

B
Work out
1. $63 - 58$
2. $300 - 188$
3. $74 - 66$
4. $5000 - 4992$
5. $306 - 199$
6. $705 - 495$
7. $6000 - 5983$
8. $2000 - 1942$
9. $3002 - 2970$
10. $107 - 88$

C
Copy and complete.
1. $604 - \square = 186$
2. $703 - \square = 274$
3. $6000 - \square = 3875$
4. $512 - \square = 197$
5. $915 - \square = 498$
6. $6018 - \square = 3993$
7. $9012 - \square = 4998$
8. $9000 - \square = 5693$
9. $7000 - \square = 3876$
10. $3008 - \square = 1985$

Now you will learn to partition into 100 s, 10 s and 1 s.

Examples $28 + 49 = 20 + 40 + 8 + 9$ $79 - 45 = 79 - 40 - 5$

$= 60 + 17$ $= 39 - 5$

$= 77$ $= 34$

A
Work out
1. $26 + 52$
2. $42 + 25$
3. $68 - 35$
4. $97 - 53$
5. $43 + 45$
6. $33 + 46$
7. $79 - 26$
8. $88 - 24$
9. $54 + 35$
10. $96 - 51$

B
Work out
1. $26 + 57$
2. $44 + 39$
3. $86 - 42$
4. $96 - 68$
5. $36 + 59$
6. $67 + 28$
7. $78 - 36$
8. $65 - 27$
9. $38 + 46$
10. $83 - 54$

C
Copy and complete.
1. $326 + \square = 578$
2. $438 + \square = 684$
3. $428 + \square = 536$
4. $174 - \square = 26$
5. $283 - \square = 64$
6. $857 - \square = 352$
7. $649 - \square = 66$
8. $736 - \square = 514$
9. $462 - \square = 141$
10. $525 - \square = 218$

MENTAL STRATEGIES (+ AND −)

On this page you will learn to identify near doubles.

Examples

$38 + 39 = (40 \times 2) - 2 - 1$
$= 80 - 3$
$= 77$

$170 + 190 = (170 \times 2) + 20$
$= 340 + 20$
$= 360$

A
Work out
1. $16 + 17$
2. $25 + 26$
3. $19 + 17$
4. $16 + 18$
5. $210 + 220$
6. $130 + 140$
7. $150 + 160$
8. $420 + 410$
9. $320 + 330$
10. $140 + 150$

B
Work out
1. $34 + 32$
2. $29 + 28$
3. $48 + 46$
4. $43 + 42$
5. $360 + 360$
6. $170 + 180$
7. $270 + 290$
8. $390 + 380$
9. $450 + 470$
10. $280 + 260$

C
Copy and complete by doubling the first number and adjusting.
1. $51 + \square = 104$
2. $72 + \square = 143$
3. $530 + \square = 1070$
4. $680 + \square = 1360$
5. $89 + \square = 177$
6. $780 + \square = 1540$
7. $870 + \square = 1750$
8. $590 + \square = 1180$
9. $660 + \square = 1310$
10. $950 + \square = 1890$

Now you will learn to add or subtract to the nearest multiple of 10 and adjust.

Examples

$46 + 29 = 46 + 30 - 1$
$= 76 - 1$
$= 75$

$94 - 29 = 94 - 30 - 1$
$= 64 - 1$
$= 63$

$85 - 31 = 85 - 30 - 1$
$= 55 - 1$
$= 54$

A
Work out
1. $62 + 9$
2. $48 - 19$
3. $36 + 21$
4. $69 - 31$
5. $54 + 19$
6. $65 - 19$
7. $63 + 31$
8. $84 - 21$
9. $48 + 19$
10. $56 - 19$

B
Work out
1. $73 + 29$
2. $67 - 19$
3. $97 + 48$
4. $85 - 29$
5. $48 + 31$
6. $93 - 51$
7. $74 + 62$
8. $176 - 61$
9. $68 + 39$
10. $154 - 49$

C
Copy and complete
1. $\square + 68 = 324$
2. $\square - 39 = 193$
3. $\square + 52 = 817$
4. $\square + 59 = 238$
5. $\square - 99 = 369$
6. $\square + 61 = 547$
7. $\square + 72 = 263$
8. $\square - 48 = 267$
9. $\square + 96 = 514$
10. $\square + 78 = 147$

MENTAL STRATEGIES (+ AND −)

On this page you will learn to use the relationship between addition and subtraction.

If you know one addition or subtraction fact, you can state three other related facts.

Example $64 + 28 = 92$ $28 + 64 = 92$ $92 - 64 = 28$ $92 - 28 = 64$

A

Copy and complete. Use the three given numbers only.

 1 $23 + 16 = 39$

$\square + \square = \square$

$39 - \square = \square$

$\square - \square = \square$

2 $46 + 17 = 63$

$\square + \square = \square$

$\square - \square = 17$

$63 - \square = \square$

B

For each of the facts below write three related facts.

1 $48 + 16 = 64$

2 $67 - 29 = 38$

3 $45 + 38 = 83$

4 $58 - 26 = 32$

5 $37 + 57 = 94$

6 $86 - 17 = 69$

7 $44 + 27 = 71$

8 $95 - 39 = 56$

9 $53 + 28 = 81$

10 $74 - 46 = 28$

C

For each set of numbers write four related + and − facts.

1 123, 214, 337

2 72, 37, 109

3 600, 170, 430

4 340, 700, 360

5 146, 219, 73

6 215, 153, 62

7 290, 510, 800

8 480, 420, 900

9 491, 327, 164

10 119, 687, 568

Now you will learn to use a variety of strategies to add several numbers.

Look for pairs that make 10 or 100. $50 + 60 + 30 + 40 + 70$ Check your answers
Start with the largest number. $8 + 16 + 5 + 3$ by adding in
Recognise an equivalent multiplication. $7 + 7 + 5 + 9 = 4 \times 7$ reverse order.

A

Add up each set of numbers.

 1 20, 30, 40

2 50, 40, 50

3 8, 6, 2

4 99, 100, 101

5 50, 40, 60

6 3, 8, 7

7 80, 30, 80

8 19, 20, 21

9 8, 4, 6

10 30, 20, 70

B

Add up each set of numbers.

1 5, 6, 4, 5

2 5, 3, 6, 7

3 6, 19, 7

4 30, 40, 30

5 40, 70, 30, 20

6 6, 5, 7, 6

7 14, 8, 9

8 2, 6, 8, 3, 4

9 10, 11, 9, 10

10 30, 40, 50, 60

C

Copy and complete.

1 $2 + \square + 6 + 8 + 7 = 28$

2 $9 + 10 + 98 + \square = 137$

3 $\square + 9 + 13 = 36$

4 $40 + 80 + 60 + \square = 250$

5 $1 + 4 + 7 + 9 + \square = 27$

6 $8 + 7 + 12 + \square = 29$

7 $5 + 7 + \square + 8 + 3 = 24$

8 $70 + 90 + \square + 30 = 230$

9 $7 + 6 + 7 + \square = 28$

10 $17 + 25 + \square + 15 = 66$

MENTAL STRATEGIES (+ AND −)

On this page you will use a variety of strategies to add or subtract pairs of numbers mentally.

A

Copy and complete the squares.

1

+	8	9	6
9	17		
7			
8			

3

+	24	32	53
15			
43			96
34			

5

+	9	21	29
62			
35			
57			

7

+	34	75	93
200			
800			
500			

2

−	8	7	9
19	11		
16			
18			9

4

−	43	26	55
78		52	
67			
99			

6

−	11	19	21
48			
24			
76			

8

−	7	9	6
104			
503			
605			

B

Write the answers only.

1 1268 + 5
2 150 − 60
3 300 − 7
4 76 − 8

5 800 + 500
6 463 + 8
7 80 + 37
8 8000 − 6

9 85 − 30
10 300 + 257
11 48 + 23
12 74 − 27

13 70 + 50
14 53 + 40
15 405 − 9
16 5001 − 4993

Add 49 to:
17 50
18 23
19 47.

Add 57 to:
20 48
21 300
22 230.

Take 71 from:
23 95
24 143
25 118.

Take 36 from:
26 63
27 81
28 55.

Make 100.
29 43 + ☐
30 92 + ☐
31 14 + ☐

C

Copy and complete by writing the missing number in the box.

1 450 + ☐ = 730
2 720 − ☐ = 430
3 4005 − ☐ = 2993
4 8·3 − ☐ = 1·8
5 ☐ + 190 = 550

6 985 − ☐ = 420
7 ☐ − 800 = 561
8 6·2 + ☐ = 10·0
9 5002 − ☐ = 4899
10 567 + ☐ = 600

11 740 − ☐ = 280
12 4·2 + ☐ = 5
13 350 + ☐ = 510
14 1231 − ☐ = 700
15 329 + ☐ = 400

On this page you will learn two informal methods for addition.

ADD LARGEST VALUE DIGITS FIRST.

Examples

```
  735       384
+  58     + 129
 ─────     ─────
  700       400
   80       100
   13        13
 ─────     ─────
  793       513
```

ADD TOO MUCH AND TAKE OFF.

Examples

```
  865                    374
+ 78                   + 163
─────                  ─────
  965  (865 + 100)       574  (374 + 200)
− 22  (100 − 78)        − 37  (200 − 163)
─────                  ─────
  943                    537
```

A

Use both methods for each sum.

1. 65 + 27
6. 74 + 36
2. 58 + 36
7. 95 + 58
3. 92 + 25
8. 127 + 65
4. 174 + 52
9. 146 + 47
5. 236 + 48
10. 289 + 94

11. Maxine has 265 story books and 93 non-fiction books. How many books does she have altogether?

B

Use both methods for each sum.

1. 225 + 47
6. 342 + 94
2. 347 + 38
7. 156 + 87
3. 553 + 75
8. 438 + 73
4. 439 + 154
9. 507 + 182
5. 606 + 178
10. 215 + 179

11. A supermarket sells 182 bottles of wine and 67 bottles of red wine. How many bottles of wine are sold altogether?

12. 145 people watch a film in the afternoon. 238 people see the film in the evening. What is the total audience?

C

Set out as in the examples. Use both methods for each sum.

1. 573 + 248
7. 807 + 673
2. 868 + 347
8. 943 + 528
3. 749 + 345
9. 876 + 367
4. 908 + 296
10. 782 + 499
5. 795 + 438
11. 648 + 553
6. 685 + 749
12. 892 + 769

13. In one day 657 adults and 394 children visit a zoo. How many people visited the zoo?

14. A school library has 686 non-fiction books and 578 story books. How many books are there in the library?

15. The Peters family went touring in their camper van. They travelled 386 miles in the first week and 278 miles in the second week. How far did they travel altogether?

On this page you will learn to use a standard method for addition.

ADD LOWEST VALUE DIGITS FIRST

Example

```
   267
+   85
─────
    12    (7 + 5)
   140    (60 + 80)
   200    (200 + 0)
─────
   352
```

CARRY BELOW THE LINE

Examples

```
   157          267          1285
+   34        +  85        +  539
─────         ─────        ──────
   191          352          1824
    1            11            11
```

A

Add the lowest value digits first.

```
1    74        5    64
   + 18          + 55

2    58        6   116
   + 37          + 68

3    62        7   148
   + 29          + 35

4    87        8   139
   + 31          + 56
```

9   Jamie has read 125 pages of his book. He has 47 more pages to read. How many pages does the book have?

10 Mia drives 63 miles on Saturday and 54 miles on Sunday. How many miles does she drive altogether?

B

Add the lowest value digits first.

```
1    163       4    491
   +  72          +  45

2    347       5    258
   +  38          + 127

3    236       6    145
   +  82          + 126
```

Add by carrying.

```
7    365      10    408
   +  84          + 184

8    149      11    752
   +  47          + 183

9    573      12    364
   +  65          + 169
```

13 There are 482 cars and 127 lorries stuck in a traffic jam. How many vehicles are held up altogether?

C

Set out as in the example and add by carrying.

```
1  487 + 268     7  297 + 124
2  357 + 194     8  569 + 375
3  268 + 185     9  1408 + 926
4  1695 + 762   10  1872 + 496
5  2259 + 478   11  634 + 278
6  366 + 269    12  1546 + 755
```

13 Rachel buys a television for £378 and a video recorder for £175. How much does she spend altogether?

14 285 men and 136 women work in a factory. How many people work there altogether?

15 Santa has 217 presents in one sack and 188 in another. How many presents does he have altogether?

On this page you will learn:

• to add several numbers.

Example

Add 26, 9, 154, 83.

Line up   26
the units.   9
            154
         + 83
         ───
           272
            12

• to add sums of money.

Example

Add £1·79 and 65p.

Line up   £1·79
decimal points. + £0·65
                 ─────
                 £2·44
                  1 1

A

Copy and complete.

1) 134   4)   45
      3   7
   + 27   +276

2) 246   5)   5
     68   64
   + 5   +558

3)   39   6)   6
    361   459
   + 8   + 32

Copy and complete.

7)   £3·75   10)   £6·17
   + £0·43   + £0·93

8)   £2·48   11)   £8·26
   + £0·09   + £0·77

9)   £4·53   12)   £5·49
   + £1·08   + £0·84

13) Rhys bought a book for £3·49. He had £0·68 left. How much money did he have before he bought the book?

B

Set out as sums and find the totals.

1) 3 + 28 + 169 + 37
2) 52 + 6 + 92 + 457
3) 43 + 348 + 7 + 64
4) 271 + 83 + 8 + 75
5) £1·26 + 65p
6) £2·48 + 37p
7) £3·65 + 94p + 31p
8) £5·76 + 85p + 13p
9) £2·54 + £1·38 + 99p
10) £3·62 + 51p + 64p

11) There were 176 adults, 9 girls and 32 boys on a plane. How many people were on the plane?

C

Set out as sums and find the totals.

1) 7 + 23 + 129 + 455 + 1676
2) 57 + 348 + 5 + 3834 + 692
3) 478 + 76 + 1319 + 4 + 85
4) 2952 + 8 + 827 + 84 + 263
5) £2·31 + 26p + 31p
6) £3·58 + 37p + 29p
7) £4·67 + £2·13 + 9p
8) £6·23 + 46p + 8p
9) £8·45 + 72p + 6p
10) £7·60 + £1·18 + 34p

11) In an election 94 people voted for Mr. Small, 2368 voted for Ms. Jenkins and 785 voted for Mrs. Peters. How many people voted?

12) Priya spent £8·73 in the grocers, 96p in the newsagents and £5·38 in the chemists. How much did she spend altogether?

On this page you will learn two informal written methods for subtraction.

COUNTING UP

```
   835
 -  67
     3   to make 70
    30   to make 100
   700   to make 800
    30   to make 830
     5   to make 835
   768
```

COMPENSATION

```
   835
 -  67
   735   (835 - 100)
 + 33    (100 - 67 = 33)
   768
```

You may find it useful to check your answers with the inverse operation.

```
   768
 +  67
   835
```

A

Use both methods for each problem.

1. 47 − 24
2. 63 − 35
3. 92 − 56
4. 67 − 29
5. 51 − 25
6. 36 − 17
7. 61 − 34
8. 72 − 44
9. 85 − 38
10. 57 − 18

11. Lewis is 27. His grandfather is 83. What is the difference in their ages?

B

Use both methods for each problem.

1. 163 − 91
2. 371 − 86
3. 542 − 67
4. 437 − 51
5. 755 − 42
6. 482 − 79
7. 796 − 45
8. 812 − 83
9. 345 − 62
10. 563 − 38

11. There are 182 children in a school. 95 are boys. How many girls are there?

12. A plane carries 317 passengers to New York and 243 passengers when it returns to London. How many fewer passengers are on the return journey?

C

Set out correctly. Use both methods for each problem.

1. 231 − 145
2. 562 − 386
3. 748 − 263
4. 483 − 138
5. 819 − 679
6. 443 − 129
7. 476 − 287
8. 837 − 552
9. 352 − 176
10. 928 − 463

11. In one week 724 people use a Leisure Centre. 569 are adults. How many are children?

12. A builder orders 535 bricks. He uses 278 of them. How many bricks are left?

13. A play is seen by 346 people on Friday and 470 people on Saturday. How many fewer people were in the audience on Friday?

On this page you will learn to use decomposition.

METHOD 1

$$835 = 800 + 30 + 5 = 800 + 20 + 15 = 700 + 120 + 15$$
$$- 67 \quad - \quad 60 + 7 \quad - \quad 60 + 7 \quad - \quad 60 + 7$$
$$\overline{700 + 60 + 8} = 768$$

METHOD 2

$$835 = 82^15 = 7^12^15$$
$$- 67 \quad - 67 \quad - 67$$
$$\overline{768}$$

You may find it useful
to check your answers
with the inverse operation

$$768$$
$$+ 67$$
$$\overline{835}$$

A

Use Method 1.

1 73
− 37

6 42
− 27

2 52
− 28

7 66
− 38

3 60
− 42

8 54
− 29

4 85
− 56

9 93
− 57

5 41
− 18

10 71
− 44

11 There are 65 people on a coach. 37 are adults. How many are children?

12 Callum has 83 stamps. 48 are British. How many are foreign?

B

Use
Method 1.

Use
Method 2.

1 182
− 57

6 347
− 76

2 237
− 92

7 162
− 95

3 348
− 83

8 290
− 81

4 426
− 68

9 618
− 52

5 350
− 74

10 472
− 94

11 A bicycle costs £195. The price is reduced by £59. What is the new price?

12 A motorist needs to drive 231 miles. He stops for petrol after 86 miles. How much further does he have to go?

C

Set out correctly and use Method 2.

1 247 − 153
7 329 − 275

2 531 − 218
8 760 − 324

3 385 − 267
9 542 − 375

4 623 − 459
10 815 − 369

5 704 − 328
11 634 − 481

6 483 − 168
12 905 − 574

13 A factory produces 655 cars. 168 are painted white. How many cars are painted other colours?

14 843 people live in Greater Wallop. 176 fewer people live in Little Wallop. How many people live in the smaller village?

On this page you will learn:

- **to find the difference between numbers with different numbers of digits.**

Example Find the difference   459   Largest number on top.
between 37 and 459   − 37   Line up the digits
‾‾‾‾
422

- **to find the difference between sums of money.**

Example Find the difference   £6·92   Line up the
between £6·92 and £3·71   − £3·71   decimal points.
‾‾‾‾‾
£3·21

A

Copy and complete.

1. 134
  − 29

2. 163
  − 47

3. 138
  − 56

4. 253
  − 72

5. 219
  − 84

6. £1·36
  − £0·24

7. £3·58
  − £1·37

8. £2·75
  − £1·42

9. £4·30
  − £3·25

10. £2·61
  − £1·34

11. There are 126 palm trees on an island. 53 are blown down in a hurricane. How many trees are left standing?

B

Set out correctly and find the differences.

1. 156 and 73
2. 69 and 248
3. 377 and 95
4. 136 and 87
5. 74 and 456
6. 319 and 36
7. £2·72 − £1·38
8. £4·61 − £2·57
9. £5·80 − £2·34
10. £3·35 − £1·69
11. £6·27 − £3·43
12. £5·53 − £3·78

13. Liam has £7·29 in his piggy bank. He takes out £1·40. How much money is left in the piggy bank?

14. A survey of visitors to a museum finds that 228 people came by car and 52 fewer people came by coach. How many people came by coach?

C

Set out correctly and find the differences.

1. 1306 and 123
2. 198 and 2451
3. 4623 and 59
4. 473 and 3510
5. 5732 and 146
6. 88 and 6145
7. £3·35 − £1·79
8. £5·70 − £2·84
9. £4·21 − £2·53
10. £6·13 − £3·17
11. £8·42 − £7·50
12. £7·50 − £2·92

13. An ice cream seller has takings of £1321 on Saturday and £548 on Sunday. What is the difference in the takings?

14. Olivia has £7·17 in her purse. She spends £3·49. How much money is left in the purse?

Example

In a magic square the sum of each row, column and diagonal is the same.

13	4	7
2	8	14
9	12	3

(↔) Rows (↔)

13 + 4 + 7 = 24
2 + 8 + 14 = 24
9 + 12 + 3 = 24

(↕) Columns (↕)

13 + 2 + 9 = 24
4 + 8 + 12 = 24
7 + 14 + 3 = 24

(↗) Diagonals (↘)

13 + 8 + 3 = 24
7 + 8 + 9 = 24

Copy and complete the following magic squares.

A

1

10	6	2
		7

2

		8
5		9
		4

3

2		6
	5	
		8

4

9	10	5
		7

B

1

	7	
6	11	10

2

	2	
	10	
4	18	

3

9		
	12	
	8	15

4

		8
		15
14		10

C

1

		7	14
13		12	
16	5	9	4
	10		

2

5	16		2
		7	13
	11	12	
17	4		

3

3		10	
	9		4
17	8	12	
6			18

4 Now try to make some magic squares of your own. Start with a 3 × 3 square.

On this page you will learn to use the relationship of multiplication to division.

Multiplication is the inverse of division.
Knowing one × or ÷ fact means that you know 3 related facts.

Example
$6 \times 4 = 24$ $4 \times 6 = 24$
$24 \div 6 = 4$ $24 \div 4 = 6$

A

Copy and complete each table.

1

×2	
4 →	8
→	10
→	18
→	14
→	16

2

×3	
4 →	12
→	30
→	21
→	27
→	18

3

×4	
4 →	16
→	32
→	24
→	44
→	28

4

×5	
4 →	20
→	45
→	25
→	40
→	35

B

Copy and complete by writing the missing number in the box.

1 ☐ × 3 = 21

2 ☐ × 4 = 36

3 4 × ☐ = 28

4 5 × ☐ = 20

5 ☐ × 1 = 5

6 ☐ × 5 = 35

7 6 × ☐ = 54

8 7 × ☐ = 42

9 ☐ × 6 = 36

10 ☐ × 8 = 24

11 8 × ☐ = 0

12 9 × ☐ = 90

Write four different × or ÷ statements for each set of numbers, as in the example above.

13 6, 8, 48

14 8, 56, 7

15 8, 9, 72

16 63, 9, 7

17 10, 120, 12

18 54, 6, 9

C

Copy and complete.

1 ☐ × 4 = 48

2 ☐ × 7 = 7

3 3 × ☐ = 75

4 9 × ☐ = 72

5 ☐ × 8 = 56

6 ☐ × 9 = 36

7 7 × ☐ = 49

8 9 × ☐ = 0

9 ☐ × 6 = 48

10 ☐ × 5 = 60

11 8 × ☐ = 88

12 4 × ☐ = 60

Copy and complete these multiplication squares.

13

×	8		
			42
4		36	
	24		21

14

×		7	
		21	15
			40
9	54		

15

×			
		54	
	40		16
	35	42	

On this page you will learn to use the vocabulary of multiplication.

A

Write a number sentence for each problem and work out the answer.

1. Multiply 8 by 2.

2. Find 12 lots of 10.

3. What is 3 times 20?

4. What is twice as big as 15?

5. What is 9 groups of 5?

6. What is 5 multiplied by 4?

7. Double thirty-five.

8. Find the product of 20 and 10.

9. There are 4 cakes in a box. There are 8 boxes. How many cakes are there?

10. David is 7. His mother is 6 times older. How old is David's mother?

11. How many days are there in 5 weeks?

12. There are 10 balloons in each packet. How many balloons are there in 4 packets?

B

Write a number sentence for each problem and work out the answer.

1. Find 7 groups of 3.

2. What is 9 times 4?

3. Multiply 25 by 8.

4. Find the product of 7 and 6.

5. What is three times as big as eight?

6. How many months are there in five years?

7. How many minutes are there in 2 hours?

8. A Junior School has 210 pupils. A Secondary School has 4 times as many. How many pupils are there at the Secondary School?

9. There are 8 apples in each bag. There are 5 bags. How many apples are there altogether?

10. Derek's dog weighs 20 kg. Derek is 4 times heavier. How much does Derek weigh?

C

| 3 | 4 | 7 | 8 | 9 |

Look at the numbers in the box.

1. Multiply the smallest number by the largest number.

2. What is the middle number times the second largest number?

3. Which number is 10 times greater than the product of the two largest numbers?

4. Find the product of the three smallest numbers.

5. Find the product of the three largest numbers.

6. What is the sum of the two smallest numbers multiplied by the total of the three largest numbers?

7. Ten different products can be made using pairs of the 5 numbers. Can you find them all?

8. Use a calculator. Find two consecutive numbers with a product of:
   a) 182   d) 1190
   b) 650   e) 1056
   c) 812   f) 1406.

On this page you will learn to use the inverse relationship of division to multiplication.

Example 1 Knowing one × or ÷ facts means that you know 3 related facts.

$8 \div 2 = 4$ $8 \div 4 = 2$
$2 \times 4 = 8$ $4 \times 2 = 8$

Example 2 $\square \div 6 = 5$ The answer is 30, because $5 \times 6 = 30$.

A

Copy and complete the tables.

1

÷2
10 → 5
16 →
→ 3
→ 9
→ 7

2

÷3
12 → 4
21 →
→ 5
→ 8
→ 6

3

÷4
32 → 8
20 →
→ 7
→ 4
→ 9

4

÷5
35 → 7
45 →
→ 6
→ 8
→ 3

B

Copy and complete.

1. $35 \div \square = 5$
2. $8 \div \square = 8$
3. $\square \div 9 = 6$
4. $\square \div 8 = 7$

5. $24 \div \square = 12$
6. $36 \div \square = 4$
7. $\square \div 3 = 9$
8. $\square \div 10 = 13$

9. $42 \div \square = 7$
10. $24 \div \square = 3$
11. $\square \div 9 = 9$
12. $\square \div 1 = 6$

13. $28 \div \square = 4$
14. $48 \div \square = 6$
15. $\square \div 6 = 5$
16. $\square \div 9 = 7$

For each of these statements write three related × or ÷ statements. See Example 1 at the top of the page.

17. $12 \div 6 = 2$
18. $3 \times 8 = 24$
19. $36 \div 4 = 9$
20. $7 \times 5 = 35$

C

Copy and complete these tables.

1

Input		Output
56	÷7	
35	÷5	
	÷1	5
	÷15	6
72		8
72		7·2

2

Input		Output
11	÷1	
175	÷25	
	÷7	20
	÷10	0·5
63		9
99		9

3

Input		Output
42	÷7	
100	÷5	
	÷9	6
	÷25	8
18		18
120		12

4. What number, when divided by 7 and then multiplied by 3, gives an answer of 18?

On this page you will learn to use the vocabulary of multiplication.

A

Write a number sentence for each problem and work out the answer.

1 Share 40 by 5.

2 Divide 16 by 2.

3 How many 10s make 90?

4 Each car can carry 3 children. How many cars are needed to carry 15 children?

5 How many 3s make 18?

6 What is 20 shared by 4?

7 What is 35 divided by 5?

8 Lucy's book has 48 pages. She has reached halfway. How many pages has she read?

9 At the start of term 4B had 36 pencils. Three weeks later a quarter of the pencils were missing. How many pencils were lost?

10 Larry saves the same amount every week. It takes him 10 weeks to save £150. How much does he save each week?

B

Write a number sentence for each problem and work out the answer.

1 Nine children share 54 conkers. How many conkers does each child receive?

2 8 cinema tickets cost £40·00. What is the cost of one ticket?

3 Robert is 60. His son is one quarter of his age. How old is Robert's son?

4 There are 3 darts in each packet.
How many packets can be made from 27 darts?

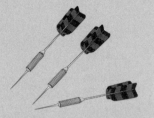

5 Five packets of sweets weigh 400g. How much does each packet weigh?

6 36 children are asked to choose their favourite colour.
1 in every 4 choose yellow.
1 in every 3 choose red.
How many children choose a different colour?

C

Write a number sentence for each problem and work out the answer.

1 900 ml of wine is shared equally between 6 glasses.
How much wine is in each glass?

2 Each box holds 16 tins of peaches.
How many boxes are needed for 80 tins?

3 3 metres of string is cut into 20 cm lengths.
How many lengths of string are there?

4 There are 222 chairs for the audience at a school concert. One sixth of the chairs are reserved. How many of the chairs are reserved?

5 From Monday to Friday Mr. Green makes the same journeys to his work and back to his home every day. At the end of the week he has driven 120 miles. How far away does he live from his work?

On this page you will learn:

- **to give a remainder.**

Examples

$26 \div 5 = 5$ remainder 1
$37 \div 10 = 3$ remainder 7

- **to divide a whole number of pounds.**

Examples

£26 ÷ 5 = £5·20, because £1 ÷ 5 = 20p
£37 ÷ 10 = £3·70, because £7 ÷ 10 = 70p

A

Copy and complete.

1. $21 = 10 \times 2 + \square$
2. $37 = 7 \times 5 + \square$
3. $73 = 7 \times 10 + \square$
4. $43 = 21 \times 2 + \square$
5. $24 = 4 \times 5 + \square$
6. $31 = 3 \times 10 + \square$
7. $28 = 9 \times 3 + \square$
8. $23 = 5 \times 4 + \square$
9. $37 = 18 \times 2 + \square$

10. $17 \div 4 = 4$ rem. $\square$
11. $16 \div 5 = 3$ rem. $\square$
12. $23 \div 2 = 11$ rem. $\square$
13. $85 \div 10 = 8$ rem. $\square$
14. $33 \div 5 = 6$ rem. $\square$
15. $29 \div 4 = 7$ rem. $\square$
16. $42 \div 5 = 8$ rem. $\square$
17. $63 \div 10 = 6$ rem. $\square$
18. $26 \div 3 = 8$ rem. $\square$

19. How many packets of 10 can be made from 76 felt tip pens. How many pens are left over?
20. Five friends share 32 marbles. How many does each person get? How many are left over?

B

Work out and give the remainder as a whole number.

1. $21 \div 2$
2. $17 \div 3$
3. $37 \div 4$
4. $113 \div 10$
5. $69 \div 5$
6. $37 \div 2$
7. $28 \div 3$
8. $23 \div 4$
9. $37 \div 5$
10. $17 \div 4$

Work out

11. £23 ÷ 2
12. £16 ÷ 5
13. £26 ÷ 4
14. £85 ÷ 10
15. £33 ÷ 5
16. £35 ÷ 2
17. £21 ÷ 4
18. £63 ÷ 10
19. £42 ÷ 5
20. £39 ÷ 4

21. How many teams of 3 can be made from 26 children? How many children are left over?

22. 4 scarecrows cost £30. How much does each scarecrow cost?

C

Work out and give the remainder as a whole number.

1. $63 \div 4$
2. $51 \div 7$
3. $67 \div 9$
4. $44 \div 6$
5. $121 \div 25$
6. $128 \div 10$
7. $72 \div 5$
8. $278 \div 25$
9. $53 \div 8$
10. $226 \div 100$

Work out

11. £76 ÷ 5
12. £57 ÷ 2
13. £631 ÷ 10
14. £55 ÷ 4
15. £92 ÷ 5
16. £7·30 ÷ 2
17. £6·00 ÷ 5
18. £7·40 ÷ 4
19. £8·50 ÷ 5
20. £14·00 ÷ 8

21. A box of 4 CDs costs £15·00. What is the cost of each CD?

22. Eight friends share the cost of a meal. The bill comes to £36·00. How much should each person pay?

23. Five train tickets cost £19·00. What does one ticket cost?

On this page you will learn to make sensible decisions about rounding up or down after division.

Examples

- How many £6 tickets can I buy with £47?

$47 \div 6 = 7$ remainder 5.

Answer: 7 tickets can be bought.

- An egg box holds 6 eggs.
How many boxes do I need to hold 47 eggs?

$47 \div 6 = 7$ remainder 5.

Answer: 8 boxes are needed.

- Each hospital ward holds fifteen patients.
How many wards are needed for 70 patients?

$70 \div 15 = 4$ remainder 10.

Answer: 5 wards are needed.

- Each dress rail in a shop holds fifteen dresses.
How many rails can be filled with 70 dresses?

$70 \div 15 = 4$ remainder 10.

Answer: 4 rails can be filled.

A

1. How many pairs of socks can be made from 27 socks?

2. Darts are sold in packs of three. How many packs can be made from 20 darts?

3. 4 oranges can be packed into a bag. How many bags can be filled with 35 oranges?

4. Katie wants to buy a toy which costs £13. She saves £2 every week. How many weeks will it take her to save the £13 she needs?

5. 4 children can sit at a table. How many tables are needed to seat the 30 children in a class.

6. Pencils cost 10p. How many can be bought for £1·38?

7. Rubbers are sold in packets of 6. How many packets does a school need to buy for a class of 32 children?

8. A car can carry 5 passengers. How many cars are needed to carry 42 passengers?

9. T shirts cost £5 each. How many can be bought for £38?

10. Each money bag holds twenty coins. How many money bags are needed for 150 coins?

B

1 Tickets for a film show cost £3. How many tickets can be bought for £35?

2 A van can carry 8 large boxes. How many vans are needed to carry 50 boxes?

3 How many 5-a-side football teams can be made up from 59 players?

4 6 children can sleep in a large tent. How many tents are needed for 75 children?

5 Chocko chocolate bars are sold in packs of 6. How many packs can be made from 52 bars?

6 10 videos can be stored on a shelf. How many shelves are needed to store 95 videos?

7 Tennis balls are sold in tubes. There are 4 balls in each tube. How many tubes can be filled from 70 balls?

8 Craig saves £3 every week. How many weeks will it take him to save £20?

9 How many complete weeks are there in 40 days?

10 Each container holds nine litres of petrol. How many containers are needed for 50 litres?

C

1 Cans of drink are sold in packs of 6. How many packs can be made from 94 cans?

2 Each tray holds sixteen flowers. How many trays are needed for 120 flowers?

3 80 cm of material is needed to make a costume. How many costumes can be made from 7 metres of material?

4 A coach can carry 35 passengers. How many coaches are needed to carry 150 passengers?

5 Pot plants cost £2·50. How many plants can be bought with £14?

6 A school hall can fit 20 chairs into one row. How many rows are needed to seat 312 parents for the school concert?

7 A baker puts his cakes onto trays which hold 8 cakes. How many trays are needed for 100 cakes?

8 There are 7 players in a netball team. There are 68 players in a netball club. How many teams can be made?

9 How many complete years are there in 70 months?

10 Albert saved £600 every month. How many months did it take him to save the £5000 he needed for his new motor cycle?

On this page you will revise the multiplication and division facts for 2, 3, 4, 5 and 10.

A

Write the answer only.

1. 8×2
2. 4×2
3. 7×2
4. 6×2
5. 9×2
6. 5×2
7. 7×3
8. 10×3
9. 8×3
10. 5×3
11. 9×3
12. 6×3
13. 6×4
14. 9×4
15. 3×4
16. 10×4
17. 7×4
18. 4×4
19. 8×5
20. 5×5
21. 7×5
22. 9×5
23. 6×5
24. 3×5
25. 4×10
26. 9×10
27. 6×10
28. 10×10
29. 8×10
30. 7×10

B

Copy and complete by writing the missing number in the box.

1. $\square \times 2 = 18$
2. $\square \times 10 = 80$
3. $6 \times \square = 18$
4. $4 \times \square = 16$
5. $\square \times 3 = 15$
6. $\square \times 5 = 45$

7. $7 \times \square = 35$
8. $6 \times \square = 12$
9. $\square \times 4 = 28$
10. $\square \times 3 = 30$
11. $7 \times \square = 70$
12. $8 \times \square = 32$

13. $\square \div 10 = 3$
14. $\square \div 2 = 8$
15. $20 \div \square = 10$
16. $27 \div \square = 9$
17. $\square \div 4 = 7$
18. $\square \div 3 = 8$

19. $100 \div \square = 10$
20. $40 \div \square = 8$
21. $\square \div 5 = 6$
22. $\square \div 4 = 9$
23. $21 \div \square = 7$
24. $20 \div \square = 5$

C

Work out the brackets first. Write the answers only.

1. $(6 \times 2) + (3 \times 10)$
2. $(8 \times 10) + (9 \times 5)$
3. $(7 \times 2) + (4 \times 10)$
4. $(9 \times 3) + (8 \times 4)$
5. $(7 \times 4) + (3 \times 5)$
6. $(10 \times 10) + (6 \times 5)$
7. $(6 \times 4) - (9 \times 2)$
8. $(5 \times 5) - (8 \times 2)$
9. $(7 \times 5) - (8 \times 3)$
10. $(8 \times 5) - (7 \times 3)$
11. $(7 \times 10) - (6 \times 3)$
12. $(9 \times 10) - (9 \times 4)$

Copy and complete the multiplication squares.

13.

×	2	3	4
10			
6			
4			

14.

×			
7			70
2	6		
9		36	

15.

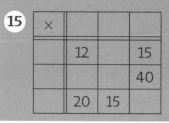

×			
	12		15
			40
	20	15	

On this page you will practise doubling and halving and learn to use partitioning to double and halve.

Examples   Double 34 = $(30 \times 2) + (4 \times 2) = 60 + 8 = 68$
Half of 76 = $(70 \div 2) + (6 \div 2) = 35 + 3 = 38$

A

Double each number.

1	8	**6**	400
2	10	**7**	35
3	15	**8**	25
4	14	**9**	45
5	17	**10**	30

Halve each number.

11	22	**16**	170
12	40	**17**	500
13	18	**18**	130
14	26	**19**	600
15	32	**20**	150

Copy and complete.

21 $23 \times 2 = (20 \times 2) + (3 \times 2)$
22 $28 \times 2 = (20 \times 2) + (8 \times 2)$
23 $37 \times 2 = (30 \times 2) + (7 \times 2)$

24 $35 \times 2 = (30 \times 2) + (5 \times 2)$
25 $46 \times 2 = (40 \times 2) + (6 \times 2)$
26 $29 \times 2 = (20 \times 2) + (9 \times 2)$

Copy and complete.

27 $48 \div 2 = (40 \div 2) + (8 \div 2)$
28 $68 \div 2 = (60 \div 2) + (8 \div 2)$
29 $52 \div 2 = (50 \div 2) + (2 \div 2)$

30 $74 \div 2 = (70 \div 2) + (4 \div 2)$
31 $86 \div 2 = (80 \div 2) + (6 \div 2)$
32 $98 \div 2 = (90 \div 2) + (8 \div 2)$

B

Write the answer only.

1	16×2
2	21×2
3	34×2
4	27×2
5	230×2
6	380×2
7	490×2
8	440×2
9	2200×2
10	3900×2
11	$42 \div 2$
12	$64 \div 2$
13	$88 \div 2$
14	$54 \div 2$
15	$760 \div 2$
16	$940 \div 2$
17	$680 \div 2$
18	$5600 \div 2$
19	$3600 \div 2$
20	$7400 \div 2$

Work out by partitioning.

21	64×2	**27**	$162 \div 2$
22	56×2	**28**	$134 \div 2$
23	78×2	**29**	$158 \div 2$
24	93×2	**30**	$178 \div 2$
25	67×2	**31**	$116 \div 2$
26	59×2	**32**	$174 \div 2$

C

Copy and complete.

1	$\square \times 2 = 62$
2	$\square \times 2 = 76$
3	$\square \times 2 = 136$
4	$\square \times 2 = 184$
5	$\square \times 2 = 1520$
6	$\square \times 2 = 1380$
7	$\square \times 2 = 7800$
8	$\square \times 2 = 1160$
9	$\square \div 2 = 92$
10	$\square \div 2 = 76$
11	$\square \div 2 = 59$
12	$\square \div 2 = 54$
13	$\square \div 2 = 770$
14	$\square \div 2 = 980$
15	$\square \div 2 = 7300$
16	$\square \div 2 = 8600$

Double by partitioning.

17	143	**21**	138
18	156	**22**	179
19	167	**23**	185
20	174	**24**	197

Halve by partitioning.

25	244	**29**	392
26	338	**30**	296
27	256	**31**	318
28	354	**32**	376

On this page you will learn to use doubling or halving to solve calculations.

Examples

MULTIPLICATION

$16 \times 4 = 16 \times 2 \times 2$
$\qquad = 32 \times 2$
$\qquad = 64$

$16 \times 5 = 16 \times 10 \div 2$
$\qquad = 160 \div 2$
$\qquad = 80$

$16 \times 20 = 16 \times 10 \times 2$
$\qquad = 160 \times 2$
$\qquad = 320$

FRACTIONS

Find one eighth of 24.

one half of $24 = 12$
one quarter of $24 = 6$
one eighth of $24 = 3$

MULTIPLES

Some multiples of 12 can be worked out by doubling.

$1 \times 12 = 12$
$2 \times 12 = 24$
$4 \times 12 = 48$
$8 \times 12 = 96$
$16 \times 12 = 192$

These multiples can be used to solve calculations.

$15 \times 12 = (16 \times 12) - (1 \times 12)$
$\qquad = 192 - 12$
$\qquad = 180$

$13 \times 12 = (8 \times 12) + (4 \times 12) + (1 \times 12)$
$\qquad = 96 + 48 + 12$
$\qquad = 96 + 60$
$\qquad = 156$

$23 \times 12 = (16 \times 12) + (8 \times 12) - (1 \times 12)$
$\qquad = 192 + 96 - 12$
$\qquad = 288 - 12$
$\qquad = 276$

A

Make the 6 times-table by doubling the 3 times-table.

1

3 times-table	6 times-table
3	6
6	
9	
12	
15	
18	
21	
24	
27	
30	60

Work out by doubling or halving the second number. Show the method used as in the examples.

2 6×4 **5** 15×4 **8** 16×5
3 8×4 **6** 23×4 **9** 24×5
4 11×4 **7** 12×5 **10** 40×5

Work out by doubling.

11 $1 \times 7 = \square$ **12** $1 \times 11 = \square$
$2 \times 7 = \square$ $2 \times 11 = \square$
$4 \times 7 = \square$ $4 \times 11 = \square$
$8 \times 7 = \square$ $8 \times 11 = \square$
$16 \times 7 = \square$ $16 \times 11 = \square$

Work out by halving.

13 $\frac{1}{2}$ of $16 = \square$ **14** $\frac{1}{2}$ of $40 = \square$
$\frac{1}{4}$ of $16 = \square$ $\frac{1}{4}$ of $40 = \square$
$\frac{1}{8}$ of $16 = \square$ $\frac{1}{8}$ of $40 = \square$

B

1 Make the 8 times-table by doubling the 4 times-table.

4 times-table	8 times-table
4	8
8	
12	
16	
20	
24	
28	
32	
36	
40	80

Work out by doubling or halving. Show the method used.

2 14×4 **5** 34×5 **8** 12×20

3 24×4 **6** 78×5 **9** 16×20

4 32×4 **7** 46×5 **10** 23×20

By doubling, work out some multiples of 13 up to 16×13. Use your multiples to work out:

11 6×13 **13** 14×13 **15** 23×13

12 9×13 **14** 19×13 **16** 26×13

Copy and complete. Use halving to find the missing numbers.

17 $\frac{1}{2}$ of $32 = \square$ **20** $\frac{1}{2}$ of $120 = \square$

$\frac{1}{4}$ of $32 = \square$ $\frac{1}{4}$ of $120 = \square$

$\frac{1}{8}$ of $32 = \square$ $\frac{1}{8}$ of $120 = \square$

18 $\frac{1}{2}$ of $200 = \square$ **21** $\frac{1}{2}$ of $40 = \square$

$\frac{1}{4}$ of $200 = \square$ $\frac{1}{4}$ of $40 = \square$

$\frac{1}{8}$ of $200 = \square$ $\frac{1}{8}$ of $40 = \square$

19 $\frac{1}{2}$ of $48 = \square$ **22** $\frac{1}{2}$ of $1000 = \square$

$\frac{1}{4}$ of $48 = \square$ $\frac{1}{4}$ of $1000 = \square$

$\frac{1}{8}$ of $48 = \square$ $\frac{1}{8}$ of $1000 = \square$

C

Work out by doubling or halving. Show the method used.

1 16×15 **4** 17×14 **7** 13×18

2 18×35 **5** 31×16 **8** 8×22

3 24×50 **6** 46×50 **9** 39×50

By doubling, work out some multiples of 25 up to 16×25. Use your multiples to work out:

10 9×25 **13** 25×25

11 15×25 **14** 22×25

12 13×25 **15** 29×25

Use halving to work out:

16 $\frac{1}{4}$ of 256 **21** $\frac{1}{8}$ of 72 **26** $\frac{1}{16}$ of 32

17 $\frac{1}{4}$ of 30 **22** $\frac{1}{8}$ of 100 **27** $\frac{1}{16}$ of 80

18 $\frac{1}{4}$ of 64 **23** $\frac{1}{8}$ of 168 **28** $\frac{1}{16}$ of 144

19 $\frac{1}{4}$ of 18 **24** $\frac{1}{8}$ of 68 **29** $\frac{1}{16}$ of 96

20 $\frac{1}{4}$ of 76 **25** $\frac{1}{8}$ of 104 **30** $\frac{1}{16}$ of 208

31 What is half of a half of 140?

32 What is half of a half of 92?

33 What is half of a quarter of 1000?

34 What is half of a quarter of 760?

Work out both problems. Use halving to solve the second problem of each pair.

35 $\frac{1}{3}$ of $24 = \square$ **38** $\frac{1}{10}$ of $300 = \square$

$\frac{1}{6}$ of $24 = \square$ $\frac{1}{20}$ of $300 = \square$

36 $\frac{1}{3}$ of $900 = \square$ **39** $\frac{1}{10}$ of $140 = \square$

$\frac{1}{6}$ of $900 = \square$ $\frac{1}{20}$ of $140 = \square$

37 $\frac{1}{3}$ of $36 = \square$ **40** $\frac{1}{10}$ of $50 = \square$

$\frac{1}{6}$ of $36 = \square$ $\frac{1}{20}$ of $50 = \square$

On this page you will practise the multiplication and division facts for 6.

A

Write out the 6 times table. Use the table to work out:

1. 5×6
2. 2×6
3. 7×6
4. 4×6
5. 0×6
6. 6×6
7. 9×6
8. 1×6
9. 10×6
10. 8×6
11. $12 \div 6$
12. $48 \div 6$
13. $24 \div 6$
14. $36 \div 6$
15. $6 \div 6$
16. $42 \div 6$
17. $18 \div 6$
18. $60 \div 6$
19. $30 \div 6$
20. $54 \div 6$
21. 6×4
22. 6×1
23. 6×7
24. 6×2
25. 6×8
26. 6×3
27. 6×9
28. 6×0
29. 6×5
30. 6×10

B

Do not use your 6 times table. Write the answers only.

1. 3×6
2. 10×6
3. 7×6
4. 9×6
5. 6×6
6. 2×6
7. 5×6
8. 0×6
9. 8×6
10. $36 \div 6$
11. $6 \div 6$
12. $60 \div 6$
13. $24 \div 6$
14. $48 \div 6$
15. $30 \div 6$
16. $54 \div 6$
17. $18 \div 6$
18. $42 \div 6$

Copy and complete.

19. $\square \times 6 = 18$
20. $\square \times 6 = 42$
21. $\square \times 6 = 24$
22. $\square \times 6 = 36$
23. $\square \times 6 = 0$
24. $\square \times 6 = 48$
25. $\square \times 6 = 30$
26. $\square \times 6 = 54$
27. $\square \div 6 = 5$
28. $\square \div 6 = 8$
29. $\square \div 6 = 10$
30. $\square \div 6 = 4$
31. $\square \div 6 = 7$
32. $\square \div 6 = 1$
33. $\square \div 6 = 9$
34. $\square \div 6 = 6$

C

Write the answers only.

1. 40×6
2. 200×6
3. 500×6
4. 70×6
5. 30×6
6. 800×6
7. 400×6
8. 700×6
9. 90×6
10. 600×6
11. $120 \div 6$
12. $600 \div 6$
13. $240 \div 6$
14. $6000 \div 6$
15. $3600 \div 6$
16. $300 \div 6$
17. $4800 \div 6$
18. $1800 \div 6$
19. $420 \div 6$
20. $5400 \div 6$

Work out by multiplying by 6 and doubling.

21. 3×12
22. 10×12
23. 5×12
24. 2×12
25. 8×12
26. 6×12
27. 4×12
28. 9×12
29. 7×12
30. 20×12

31. There are six chairs in every stack. There are 24 stacks. How many chairs are there?

32. Eggs are packed into boxes of 6. How many boxes are needed for 96 eggs?

On this page you will practise the multiplication and division facts for 7.

A

Write out the 7 times table. Use the table to work out:

1. 3×7
2. 2×7
3. 5×7
4. 1×7
5. 8×7
6. 0×7
7. 7×7
8. 4×7
9. 9×7
10. 6×7
11. $28 \div 7$
12. $14 \div 7$
13. $70 \div 7$
14. $7 \div 7$
15. $42 \div 7$
16. $21 \div 7$
17. $63 \div 7$
18. $49 \div 7$
19. $35 \div 7$
20. $56 \div 7$
21. 7×2
22. 7×5
23. 7×9
24. 7×1
25. 7×3
26. 7×6
27. 7×0
28. 7×4
29. 7×10
30. 7×8

B

Do not use your 7 times table. Write the answers only.

1. 5×7
2. 2×7
3. 4×7
4. 0×7
5. 9×7
6. 7×7
7. 8×7
8. 6×7
9. 10×7
10. $21 \div 7$
11. $70 \div 7$
12. $56 \div 7$
13. $14 \div 7$
14. $42 \div 7$
15. $35 \div 7$
16. $63 \div 7$
17. $28 \div 7$
18. $49 \div 7$

Copy and complete.

19. $\square \times 7 = 14$
20. $\square \times 7 = 35$
21. $\square \times 7 = 56$
22. $\square \times 7 = 21$
23. $\square \times 7 = 42$
24. $\square \times 7 = 28$
25. $\square \times 7 = 63$
26. $\square \times 7 = 49$
27. $\square \div 7 = 3$
28. $\square \div 7 = 7$
29. $\square \div 7 = 2$
30. $\square \div 7 = 5$
31. $\square \div 7 = 9$
32. $\square \div 7 = 6$
33. $\square \div 7 = 1$
34. $\square \div 7 = 8$

C

Write the answers only.

1. 20×7
2. 50×7
3. 80×7
4. 400×7
5. 200×7
6. 70×7
7. 300×7
8. 90×7
9. 600×7
10. 800×7
11. $490 \div 7$
12. $280 \div 7$
13. $140 \div 7$
14. $5600 \div 7$
15. $350 \div 7$
16. $2100 \div 7$
17. $420 \div 7$
18. $630 \div 7$
19. $7000 \div 7$
20. $4900 \div 7$

Work out by multiplying by 7 and doubling.

21. 5×14
22. 2×14
23. 6×14
24. 9×14
25. 3×14
26. 8×14
27. 30×14
28. 4×14
29. 7×14
30. 60×14

31. How many weeks are there in 224 days?

32. Each minibus can carry 13 passengers. How many passengers can be carried in 7 minibuses?

33. What number is seven times greater than seven times seven?

On this page you will practise the multiplication and division facts for 8.

A

Write out the 8 times table. Use the table to work out:

1. 5×8
2. 2×8
3. 10×8
4. 4×8
5. 9×8
6. 7×8
7. 1×8
8. 8×8
9. 0×8
10. 6×8
11. $24 \div 8$
12. $80 \div 8$
13. $64 \div 8$
14. $16 \div 8$
15. $48 \div 8$
16. $8 \div 8$
17. $40 \div 8$
18. $72 \div 8$
19. $32 \div 8$
20. $56 \div 8$
21. 8×3
22. 8×6
23. 8×2
24. 8×0
25. 8×10
26. 8×1
27. 8×4
28. 8×9
29. 8×5
30. 8×7

B

Do not use your 8 times table. Write the answers only.

1. 3×8
2. 10×8
3. 6×8
4. 0×8
5. 9×8
6. 4×8
7. 7×8
8. 1×8
9. 8×8
10. $40 \div 8$
11. $80 \div 8$
12. $24 \div 8$
13. $72 \div 8$
14. $48 \div 8$
15. $8 \div 8$
16. $64 \div 8$
17. $32 \div 8$
18. $56 \div 8$

Copy and complete.

19. $\square \times 8 = 40$
20. $\square \times 8 = 24$
21. $\square \times 8 = 48$
22. $\square \times 8 = 16$
23. $\square \times 8 = 72$
24. $\square \times 8 = 56$
25. $\square \times 8 = 32$
26. $\square \times 8 = 64$
27. $\square \div 8 = 3$
28. $\square \div 8 = 7$
29. $\square \div 8 = 1$
30. $\square \div 8 = 4$
31. $\square \div 8 = 8$
32. $\square \div 8 = 6$
33. $\square \div 8 = 5$
34. $\square \div 8 = 9$

C

Write the answers only.

1. 40×8
2. 20×8
3. 700×8
4. 300×8
5. 50×8
6. 200×8
7. 90×8
8. 500×8
9. 80×8
10. 600×8
11. $320 \div 8$
12. $160 \div 8$
13. $4800 \div 8$
14. $240 \div 8$
15. $3200 \div 8$
16. $640 \div 8$
17. $800 \div 8$
18. $5600 \div 8$
19. $720 \div 8$
20. $4000 \div 8$

Work out by multiplying by 8 and doubling.

21. 2×16
22. 5×16
23. 7×16
24. 3×16
25. 9×16
26. 6×16
27. 8×16
28. 4×16
29. 20×16
30. 30×16

31. There are eight cakes in each box. How many boxes are needed for 208 cakes?

32. A lorry travels the same route eight times every day. The route is 29 miles long. How far does the lorry travel in one day?

On this page you will practise the multiplication and division facts for 9.

A

Write out the 9 times table. Use the table to work out:

1. 3×9
2. 10×9
3. 7×9
4. 1×9
5. 5×9
6. 2×9
7. 6×9
8. 9×9
9. 0×9
10. 8×9
11. $36 \div 9$
12. $63 \div 9$
13. $18 \div 9$
14. $45 \div 9$
15. $90 \div 9$
16. $9 \div 9$
17. $81 \div 9$
18. $27 \div 9$
19. $72 \div 9$
20. $54 \div 9$
21. 9×5
22. 9×2
23. 9×1
24. 9×7
25. 9×4
26. 9×0
27. 9×10
28. 9×3
29. 9×6
30. 9×8

B

Do not use your 9 times table. Write the answers only.

1. 4×9
2. 8×9
3. 1×9
4. 10×9
5. 0×9
6. 6×9
7. 9×9
8. 5×9
9. 7×9
10. $27 \div 9$
11. $45 \div 9$
12. $81 \div 9$
13. $54 \div 9$
14. $18 \div 9$
15. $36 \div 9$
16. $63 \div 9$
17. $90 \div 9$
18. $72 \div 9$

Copy and complete.

19. $\square \times 9 = 54$
20. $\square \times 9 = 36$
21. $\square \times 9 = 81$
22. $\square \times 9 = 90$
23. $\square \times 9 = 27$
24. $\square \times 9 = 72$
25. $\square \times 9 = 45$
26. $\square \times 9 = 63$
27. $\square \div 9 = 4$
28. $\square \div 9 = 10$
29. $\square \div 9 = 8$
30. $\square \div 9 = 3$
31. $\square \div 9 = 7$
32. $\square \div 9 = 1$
33. $\square \div 9 = 6$
34. $\square \div 9 = 9$

C

Write the answers only.

1. 30×9
2. 50×9
3. 70×9
4. 20×9
5. 300×9
6. 400×9
7. 80×9
8. 600×9
9. 500×9
10. 900×9
11. $270 \div 9$
12. $450 \div 9$
13. $180 \div 9$
14. $810 \div 9$
15. $360 \div 9$
16. $5400 \div 9$
17. $9000 \div 9$
18. $720 \div 9$
19. $1800 \div 9$
20. $6300 \div 9$

Work out by multiplying by 9 and doubling.

21. 3×18
22. 6×18
23. 2×18
24. 30×18
25. 5×18
26. 8×18
27. 20×18
28. 4×18
29. 9×18
30. 7×18

31. A multi storey car park has 9 levels. There are 36 parking spaces on each level. How many cars can park in the car park?

32. A school buys some tennis rackets for £153. Each racket costs £9. How many rackets does the school buy?

On this page you will learn to multiply a number by 9 or 11.

Examples

$15 × 9 = (15 × 10) − 15$
$= 150 − 15$
$= 135$

$15 × 11 = (15 × 10) + 15$
$= 150 + 15$
$= 165$

$18 × 19 = (18 × 20) − 18$
$= 360 − 18$
$= 342$

 A

Work out

1. $4 × 9$
2. $3 × 11$
3. $6 × 9$
4. $5 × 11$
5. $8 × 9$
6. $7 × 11$
7. $9 × 9$
8. $6 × 11$
9. $7 × 9$
10. $8 × 11$

B

Work out

1. $12 × 9$
2. $13 × 11$
3. $16 × 9$
4. $17 × 11$
5. $13 × 9$
6. $15 × 11$
7. $19 × 9$
8. $12 × 11$
9. $15 × 9$
10. $19 × 11$

C

Copy and complete.

1. $\square ÷ 19 = 7$
2. $\square ÷ 21 = 6$
3. $\square ÷ 19 = 11$
4. $\square ÷ 21 = 9$
5. $\square ÷ 19 = 14$
6. $\square ÷ 21 = 13$
7. $\square ÷ 19 = 16$
8. $\square ÷ 21 = 18$
9. $\square ÷ 19 = 19$
10. $\square ÷ 21 = 21$

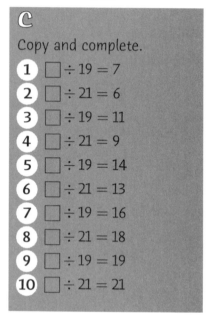

● Now you will learn to multiply a two-digit number by partitioning.

Examples

$34 × 3 = (30 × 3) + (4 × 3)$
$= 90 + 12$
$= 112$

$26 × 4 = (20 × 4) + (6 × 4)$
$= 80 + 24$
$= 104$

 A

Copy and complete.

1. $14 × 2 = (10 × 2) + (4 × 2) = \square + \square = \square$
2. $13 × 5 = (10 × 5) + (3 × 5) = \square + \square = \square$
3. $17 × 2 = (10 × 2) + (7 × 2) = \square + \square = \square$
4. $16 × 5 = (10 × 5) + (6 × 5) = \square + \square = \square$
5. $23 × 2 = (20 × 2) + (3 × 2) = \square + \square = \square$
6. $19 × 5 = (10 × 5) + (9 × 5) = \square + \square = \square$
7. $26 × 2 = (20 × 2) + (6 × 2) = \square + \square = \square$
8. $22 × 5 = (20 × 5) + (2 × 5) = \square + \square = \square$
9. $32 × 2 = (30 × 2) + (2 × 2) = \square + \square = \square$
10. $25 × 5 = (20 × 5) + (5 × 5) = \square + \square = \square$

B

Work out

1. $12 × 3$
2. $13 × 4$
3. $19 × 3$
4. $17 × 4$
5. $23 × 3$
6. $22 × 4$
7. $27 × 3$
8. $29 × 4$
9. $35 × 3$
10. $34 × 4$

C

Copy and complete.

1. $\square ÷ 4 = 32$
2. $\square ÷ 5 = 46$
3. $\square ÷ 6 = 37$
4. $\square ÷ 7 = 16$
5. $\square ÷ 8 = 25$
6. $\square ÷ 9 = 28$
7. $\square ÷ 4 = 39$
8. $\square ÷ 5 = 53$
9. $\square ÷ 6 = 48$
10. $\square ÷ 7 = 23$

On this page you will practise multiplying a multiple of 10 by a single-digit number.

Examples $40 \times 6 = 240$ $70 \times 3 = 210$ $80 \times 4 = 320$

A

Work out

1. 20×3
2. 40×2
3. 50×4
4. 30×5
5. 40×3
6. 20×5
7. 50×2
8. 30×3
9. 40×4
10. 30×2
11. 50×5
12. 30×4

B

Copy and complete.

1. $50 \times 3 = \square$
2. $30 \times 8 = \square$
3. $90 \times 4 = \square$
4. $70 \times 5 = \square$
5. $30 \times \square = 90$
6. $20 \times \square = 100$
7. $40 \times \square = 280$
8. $70 \times \square = 210$
9. $\square \times 9 = 180$
10. $\square \times 5 = 400$
11. $\square \times 4 = 240$
12. $\square \times 6 = 300$

C

Copy and complete the tables.

1

×6	
90 →	540
→	360
→	480
50 →	
30 →	

2

×7	
60 →	
70 →	
→	350
→	560
→	280

3

×8	
80 →	
→	480
30 →	
→	720
→	560

4

×9	
50 →	
80 →	
→	360
→	810
70 →	

- Now you will practise multiplying a two-digit number by a single-digit number.

Examples $14 \times 4 = (10 \times 4) + (4 \times 4) = 40 + 16 = 56$

A

Work out

1. 12×2
2. 11×5
3. 21×4
4. 13×3
5. 14×2
6. 22×3
7. 12×4
8. 34×2
9. 12×3
10. 42×2
11. 23×3
12. 22×4

B

Copy and complete.

1. $16 \times 2 = \square$
2. $23 \times 5 = \square$
3. $18 \times 4 = \square$
4. $15 \times 3 = \square$
5. $13 \times \square = 65$
6. $25 \times \square = 50$
7. $17 \times \square = 51$
8. $19 \times \square = 38$
9. $\square \times 4 = 56$
10. $\square \times 5 = 110$
11. $\square \times 3 = 75$
12. $\square \times 4 = 84$

C

Copy and complete the tables.

1

×6	
43 →	
57 →	
38 →	
→	186
→	252

2

×7	
24 →	
19 →	
36 →	
→	497
→	301

3

×8	
35 →	
48 →	
63 →	
→	440
→	192

4

×9	
18 →	
37 →	
72 →	
→	459
→	396

On this page you will practise:

- **doubling multiples of 5.**

Examples

Double 45 = (40 × 2) + (5 × 2)
= 80 + 10
= 90

Double 235 = (200 × 2) + (30 × 2) + (5 × 2)
= 400 + 60 + 10
= 470

- **halving multiples of 10.**

Example

Half of 150 = (100 ÷ 2) + (50 ÷ 2)
= 50 + 25
= 75

A

Double these numbers.

1	20	**6**	50
2	30	**7**	70
3	35	**8**	60
4	40	**9**	15
5	45	**10**	65

Halve these numbers.

11	30	**16**	90
12	80	**17**	60
13	50	**18**	20
14	70	**19**	100
15	40	**20**	200

21 How much is double 25p?

22 What is twice £150?

23 How much is half of £200?

24 Find half of 120 pence.

25 Double £1·20.

26 Halve £400.

B

Work out

1	25 × 2	**7**	140 ÷ 2
2	35 × 2	**8**	70 ÷ 2
3	40 × 2	**9**	110 ÷ 2
4	55 × 2	**10**	180 ÷ 2
5	80 × 2	**11**	130 ÷ 2
6	85 × 2	**12**	150 ÷ 2

Copy and complete.

13 ☐ × 2 = 40

14 ☐ × 2 = 90

15 ☐ × 2 = 130

16 ☐ × 2 = 160

17 ☐ ÷ 2 = 35

18 ☐ ÷ 2 = 60

19 ☐ ÷ 2 = 95

20 ☐ ÷ 2 = 65

21 36 ☐ 2 = 72

22 54 ☐ 2 = 27

23 88 ☐ 2 = 44

24 79 ☐ 2 = 158

C

Copy and complete the tables.

1

Double
75 → 150
125 →
160 →
255 →
380 →
475 →

3

Halve
260 → 130
420 →
770 →
690 →
580 →
850 →

2

Double
95 → 190
→ 340
→ 630
→ 870
→ 520
→ 790

4

Halve
320 → 160
→ 235
→ 370
→ 455
→ 315
→ 445

Write down the number which is:

5 double 5 lots of 17.

6 double 33 fives.

7 twice three times 9.

8 half of a half of 540.

9 half of a quarter of 680.

10 half of a tenth of 120.

On this page you will practise multiplying a number by 10 or 100.

Examples $184 \times 10 = 1840$ $32 \times 100 = 3200$

A

Work out

1. 3×10
2. 7×10
3. 5×10
4. 8×10
5. 9×10
6. 9×100
7. 4×100
8. 8×100
9. 5×100
10. 7×100

B

Copy and complete the tables.

1

×10
42 → 420
315 →
→ 660
→ 4290
→ 540
218 →
→ 6720
51 →
196 →
→ 5370

2

×100
16 → 1600
43 →
9 →
→ 2500
→ 7100
→ 400
57 →
→ 3200
86 →
→ 6400

C

Copy and complete.

1. $253 \times 10 = \square$
2. $84 \times 100 = \square$
3. $108 \times 10 = \square$
4. $246 \times 100 = \square$
5. $35 \times \square = 3500$
6. $530 \times \square = 5300$
7. $671 \times \square = 6710$
8. $\square \times 100 = 43\,000$
9. $\square \times 10 = 1270$
10. $\square \times 100 = 10\,200$

Now you will practise dividing a multiple of 1000 by 10 or 100.

Examples $4000 \div 10 = 400$ $7000 \div 100 = 70$

A

Work out

1. $200 \div 10$
2. $70 \div 10$
3. $400 \div 10$
4. $800 \div 10$
5. $900 \div 10$
6. $700 \div 100$
7. $300 \div 100$
8. $600 \div 100$
9. $500 \div 100$
10. $900 \div 100$

B

Copy and complete the tables.

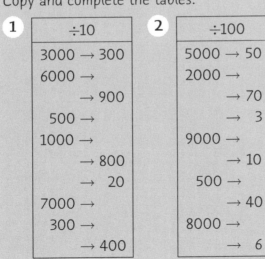

1

÷10
3000 → 300
6000 →
→ 900
500 →
1000 →
→ 800
→ 20
7000 →
300 →
→ 400

2

÷100
5000 → 50
2000 →
→ 70
→ 3
9000 →
→ 10
500 →
→ 40
8000 →
→ 6

C

Copy and complete.

1. $3200 \div 10 = \square$
2. $7000 \div 100 = \square$
3. $1800 \div 100 = \square$
4. $5000 \div 10 = \square$
5. $2300 \div \square = 230$
6. $6700 \div \square = 67$
7. $4600 \div \square = 460$
8. $719 \times \square = 71\,900$
9. $\square \div 100 = 40$
10. $\square \div 10 = 78$

64 INFORMAL METHOD FOR MULTIPLICATION

On this page you will learn the grid method for multiplication.

Example 1 24×6

×	20	4	
6	120	24	= 144

Example 2 135×7

×	100	30	5	
7	700	210	35	= 945

A

Copy and complete.

1 × 10 4 / 2 ☐ ☐ =

2 × 10 5 / 3 ☐ ☐ =

3 × 10 7 / 5 ☐ ☐ =

4 × 10 3 / 4 ☐ ☐ =

5 × 10 9 / 5 ☐ ☐ =

6 × 10 8 / 3 ☐ ☐ =

7 × 20 4 / 4 ☐ ☐ =

8 × 20 9 / 2 ☐ ☐ =

9 × 20 8 / 5 ☐ ☐ =

10 × 20 5 / 4 ☐ ☐ =

11 × 30 3 / 5 ☐ ☐ =

12 × 30 6 / 3 ☐ ☐ =

B

Copy and complete.

1 × 20 4 / 2 ☐ ☐

2 × 20 6 / 5 ☐ ☐

3 × 10 3 / 6 ☐ ☐

4 × 20 1 / 7 ☐ ☐

5 × 20 8 / 4 ☐ ☐

6 × 40 7 / 3 ☐ ☐

7 × 30 5 / 7 ☐ ☐

8 × 40 7 / 5 ☐ ☐

Use the grid method.

9 24×8 **11** 43×7 **13** 67×4 **15** 24×7

10 32×9 **12** 33×8 **14** 45×9 **16** 36×6

C

Copy and complete.

1 × 100 20 7 / 4 ☐ ☐ ☐ =

2 × 100 20 9 / 5 ☐ ☐ ☐ =

3 × 200 10 4 / 7 ☐ ☐ ☐ =

4 × 100 50 3 / 8 ☐ ☐ ☐ =

5 × 200 20 4 / 6 ☐ ☐ ☐ =

6 × 100 60 4 / 9 ☐ ☐ ☐ =

Use the grid method.

7 138×7 **9** 162×6 **11** 248×6 **13** 288×5 **15** 196×7 **17** 375×6

8 257×8 **10** 325×9 **12** 167×9 **14** 469×8 **16** 285×9 **18** 583×8

On this page you will learn a standard written method for multiplication.

Examples METHOD 1   METHOD 2 (with carries)

```
              24              37                 24          37
            ×  8            ×  4               ×  8        ×  4
(20 × 8)    160   (30 × 4)   120              ───         ───
(4 × 8)      32   (7 × 4)     28               192         148
            ───             ───                  3           2
            192             148
```

A

Work out

1 (10 × 2) + (7 × 2)

2 (20 × 3) + (3 × 3)

3 (10 × 4) + (5 × 4)

4 (20 × 5) + (1 × 5)

5 (20 × 2) + (6 × 2)

6 (10 × 5) + (9 × 5)

Copy and complete.

7
```
              18
            ×  3
            ──
10 × 3
8 × 3       ──
```

8
```
              46
            ×  5
            ──
40 × 5
6 × 5       ──
```

9
```
              28
            ×  4
            ──
20 × 4
8 × 4       ──
```

Check your answers with an addition.

Examples

1. 17 + 17 = ☐

2. 23 + 23 + 23 = ☐

B

Use Method 1.

```
1    67        6    59
   ×  2          ×  3

2    26        7    83
   ×  4          ×  2

3    32        8    28
   ×  6          ×  5

4    41        9    14
   ×  7          ×  8

5    39       10    37
   ×  5          ×  4
```

Use Method 2.

```
11   46       16    34
   ×  4          ×  6

12   73       17    53
   ×  5          ×  7

13   25       18    26
   ×  8          ×  8

14   19       19    64
   ×  9          ×  5

15   58       20    39
   ×  3          ×  4
```

C

Copy and complete.

1
```
              368
            ×   5
300 × 5
60 × 5
8 × 5       ──
```

2
```
              629
            ×   4
600 × 4
20 × 4
9 × 4       ──
```

Use Method 2 only.

```
3    137       7    168
   ×   4          ×   7

4    245       8    598
   ×   7          ×   3

5    157       9    436
   ×   6          ×   8

6    325      10    158
   ×   9          ×   9
```

Set out correctly and use Method 2.

11 318 × 6   14 329 × 7

12 182 × 8   15 246 × 9

13 473 × 5   16 397 × 8

On this page you will learn an informal method for division.

Examples

$86 \div 5$

Approximate $50 \div 5 = 10$

$100 \div 5 = 20$

$86 \div 5$ lies between 10 and 20

Calculate
```
      86
   -  50   (10 × 5)
      36
   -  35   (7 × 5)
       1
```
Answer 17 remainder 1

$231 \div 6$

Approximate $180 \div 6 = 30$

$240 \div 6 = 40$

$231 \div 6$ lies between 30 and 40.

Calculate
```
      231
    -  60   (10 × 6)
      171
    - 120   (20 × 6)
       51
    -  48   (8 × 6)
        3
```
Answer 38 remainder 3

A

Work out

1. $26 \div 2$
2. $36 \div 3$
3. $64 \div 4$
4. $75 \div 5$

5. $56 \div 4$
6. $65 \div 5$
7. $34 \div 2$
8. $48 \div 3$

9. $90 \div 5$
10. $76 \div 4$
11. $45 \div 3$
12. $38 \div 2$

13. $52 \div 4$
14. $57 \div 3$
15. $85 \div 5$
16. $72 \div 4$

B

Work out

1. $42 \div 3$
2. $66 \div 4$
3. $37 \div 2$
4. $73 \div 5$
5. $110 \div 6$
6. $122 \div 7$
7. $149 \div 9$
8. $71 \div 4$
9. $124 \div 8$
10. $95 \div 6$
11. $94 \div 5$
12. $90 \div 7$
13. $163 \div 9$
14. $55 \div 3$
15. $75 \div 6$
16. $143 \div 8$

17. Jasper wants to buy a ring for £116. He has saved one quarter of the amount needed. How much more does he need to save?

C

Work out

1. $154 \div 6$
2. $248 \div 7$
3. $221 \div 8$
4. $313 \div 9$
5. $199 \div 6$
6. $323 \div 7$
7. $378 \div 8$
8. $388 \div 9$
9. $265 \div 6$
10. $401 \div 7$
11. $437 \div 8$
12. $591 \div 9$
13. $347 \div 6$
14. $513 \div 7$
15. $516 \div 8$
16. $700 \div 9$

17. There are eight rolls in a packet. How many packets can be made from 312 rolls?

18. Footballs cost £7. How many can a school buy for £196?

19. Six boxes contain 216 apples altogether. How many apples are there in one box?

20. There are 468 bricks arranged in nine equal piles. How many bricks are in each pile?

On this page you will learn to use a standard written method for division.

Examples

$96 \div 6$

$$6\overline{)96}$$
$-\underline{60}$ (10×6)
   36
   $\underline{36}$ (6×6)
    0

Answer 16

$196 \div 6$

$$6\overline{)196}$$
$-\underline{180}$ (30×6)
   16
   $\underline{12}$ (2×6)
    4

Answer 32 remainder 4

You may find it useful to check your answer with the inverse operation.
Example $96 \div 6 = 16$

    16
$\times$ 6
  $\underline{96}$
    3

A

Work out

1. $24 \div 2$
2. $32 \div 2$
3. $28 \div 2$
4. $38 \div 2$

5. $39 \div 3$
6. $45 \div 3$
7. $54 \div 3$
8. $51 \div 3$

9. $48 \div 4$
10. $64 \div 4$
11. $76 \div 4$
12. $56 \div 4$

13. $65 \div 5$
14. $75 \div 5$
15. $90 \div 5$
16. $85 \div 5$

17. How many 3s are there in 42?
18. What is 72 divided by 4?
19. Share 80 by 5.
20. Divide 34 by 2.

B

Work out

1. $36 \div 2$
2. $95 \div 5$
3. $96 \div 6$
4. $98 \div 7$
5. $69 \div 3$
6. $96 \div 8$
7. $136 \div 4$
8. $126 \div 9$
9. $120 \div 5$
10. $108 \div 6$
11. $102 \div 3$
12. $136 \div 8$
13. $112 \div 4$
14. $153 \div 9$
15. $145 \div 5$
16. $154 \div 7$

17. Cakes are sold in packets of 8. How many packets are made up from 168 cakes?

18. 150 children are divided equally into 6 classes. How many children are there in each class?

19. A school buys 180 pencils. One quarter of the pencils are used. How many are left?

C

Work out

1. $114 \div 6$
2. $147 \div 7$
3. $176 \div 8$
4. $162 \div 9$
5. $126 \div 6$
6. $105 \div 7$
7. $149 \div 8$
8. $225 \div 9$
9. $162 \div 6$
10. $161 \div 7$
11. $232 \div 8$
12. $198 \div 9$
13. $144 \div 6$
14. $217 \div 7$
15. $191 \div 8$
16. $306 \div 9$

17. A packet of sweets weighs 224 g. Each sweet weighs 8 g. How many sweets are there in the packet?

18. 7 oil drums contain 315 litres. How much oil is there in each drum?

19. One seventh of the 308 children in a school come by bus. How many children come to school in other ways?

On this page you will learn to recognise the operation in a number sentence.

Examples

78 ☐ 49 = 29   The missing sign is −.   20 ☐ 6 = 120   The missing sign is ×.

54 ☐ 3 = 18   The missing sign is ÷.   32 ☐ 19 = 51   The missing sign is +.

A

Copy and complete.

1 63 ☐ 27 = 90

2 50 ☐ 11 = 39

3 13 ☐ 10 = 130

4 26 ☐ 12 = 14

5 55 ☐ 5 = 11

6 28 ☐ 2 = 14

7 124 ☐ 70 = 194

8 23 ☐ 2 = 46

B

Copy and complete.

1 56 ☐ 48 = 104

2 84 ☐ 2 = 42

3 275 ☐ 85 = 360

4 100 ☐ 47 = 53

5 20 ☐ 6 = 120

6 36 ☐ 3 = 12

7 12 ☐ 4 = 48

8 68 ☐ 34 = 34

C

Copy and complete.

1 364 ☐ 87 = 277

2 16 ☐ 9 = 144

3 50 ☐ 7·5 = 42·5

4 142 ☐ 76 = 218

5 35 ☐ 24 = 840

6 126 ☐ 18 = 7

7 28 ☐ 3·6 = 31·6

8 26 ☐ 4 = 6·5

● **Now you will learn to make up stories to match number sentences.**

Example   78 − 49 = 29.   Sarah had 78p. She spent 49p. She had 29p left.

A

Make up a story to match each number sentence.

1 12 + 9 = 21

2 24 ÷ 2 = 12

3 9 × 5 = 45

4 36 − 14 = 22

5 32 + 32 = 64

6 60 ÷ 10 = 6

7 18 × 10 = 180

8 50 − 13 = 37

B

Make up a story to match each number sentence.

1 39 + 26 = 65

2 120 ÷ 5 = 24

3 25 × 3 = 75

4 57 − 36 = 21

5 267 + 49 = 316

6 74 ÷ 2 = 37

7 70 × 4 = 280

8 100 − 23 = 77

C

Make up a story to match each number sentence.

1 7·8 + 5·4 = 13·2

2 282 ÷ 6 = 47

3 35 × 28 = 980

4 637 − 69 = 568

5 4 ÷ 8 = 0.5

6 18 × 9 = 162

7 1·6 + 0·9 = 2·5

8 8 − 1·6 = 6·4

On this page you will learn to find examples that match a general statement.

Example

The sums of the opposite corners of any number square are equal.

5 6 7
8 9 10 $5 + 13 = 7 + 11$
11 12 13

1 2 3 4
5 6 7 8 $1 + 16 = 4 + 13$
9 10 11 12
13 14 15 16

 A

Find two examples to match each of these general statements.

1 The sum of two odd numbers is even.

2 Multiples of 4 end in a 0, 2, 4, 6 or 8.

$51 + 75 = ?$

3 Any odd number is double a number add 1.

4 Doubling and doubling again is the same as multiplying by 4.

5 The perimeter of a square is 4 times the length.

6 Halfway between any two multiples of 10 is a multiple of 5.

B

Find three examples to match each of these general statements.

1 The sum of three odd numbers is odd.

2 Multiples of 6 end in a 0, 2, 4, 6 or 8.

3 Multiplying a number by 10 moves every digit one place to the left.

4 To multiply by 5, multiply by 10 and halve the answer.

5 The perimeter of a rectangle is twice the width
   plus twice the length.

6 Halfway between any two multiples of 6
   is a multiple of 3.

30   ?   60

C

Find three examples to match each of these general statements.

1 The sum of four odd numbers is even.

$3 + 7 + 9 + 17 = ?$

2 Multiples of 8 end in a 0, 2, 4, 6 or 8.

3 Dividing a number by 10 moves every digit one place to the right.

4 To multiply by 20, multiply by 10 and double the answer.

5 The number of lines of reflective symmetry in a regular polygon is equal to the number of
   sides of the polygon.

6 Halfway between any two multiples of 8 is a multiple of 4.

On these pages you will learn:

- **to choose the operation or operations needed to solve word problems.**

- **to decide whether the calculation will be done mentally or on paper.**

- **to use all four operations to solve the problems.**

Some of the problems need one operation only. Some need more than one.

David has 28 toys. Lindsey has 16.
How many toys do they have altogether?

$$28 + 16 = 44$$

They have 44 toys altogether.

David has 26 crayons. Lindsey has 15 more than David. How many do they have altogether?

$$26 + 15 = 41$$
$$41 + 26 = 67$$

They have 67 crayons altogether.

In each section read the problems and decide:

a) what operations are needed.
b) whether the calculation will be done mentally or on paper.

Then solve the problems.

A

1. Chris is 17. Sarah is 24 years older. How old is Sarah?

2. There are 34 passengers on a bus. 15 get off. How many passengers are there now on the bus?

3. There were eight teams at a 5-a-side football tournament.
How many players were there?

4. There were 36 sweets in 3 packets. How many sweets were there in one packet?

5. Matthew's book has 65 pages. He is on page 17. How many more pages are there till the end of the book?

6. There were three piles of 8 bricks. How many bricks were there?

7. Claire has 46 books on her top shelf and 9 less on her bottom shelf. How many books does she have altogether?

8. Twenty-six children sit in two equal rows. How many children are in each row?

9. During the football season Joe's team scored 64 goals. Harry's team only scored half as many. How many goals were scored by the two teams altogether?

10. A class of 30 children were asked what was their favourite colour. Half the children chose red. 7 children chose blue. How many children chose a different colour?

B

1. How many legs are there on 15 chairs?

2. Laura ran round the field in 51 seconds. Rebecca was 13 seconds quicker. What was Rebecca's time?

3. 67 parents voted for a longer school lunchtime. 54 voted against. How many parents voted?

4. 48 children sit in six equal rows. How many children are there in each row?

5. Emma has 35 fish in her pond. James has 28 more fish than Emma. How many fish do they have altogether?

6. Salim had 84 conkers. He gave one quarter of them to his brother. How many did he have left?

7. There were 86 people in a swimming pool. 28 got out. 43 went in. How many were there then in the pool?

8. Three shelves each had 25 books and there were nine books on another shelf. How many books were there altogether?

9. There are twenty stacks of 6 chairs and fourteen stacks of 4 chairs. How many chairs are there altogether?

10. Sixty children entered a fancy dress competition. One quarter of them came as witches. How many children wore a different costume?

C

1. A baker made 143 doughnuts. He sold 87. How many were left?

2. There are 19 more boys than there are girls in a school. There are 138 girls. How many children are there in the School?

3. A school ordered 5 crates of milk. There were 32 cartons in each crate. How many cartons of milk were delivered?

4. A cafe needed 300 paper cups. There were 60 cups in one packet. How many packets did they need to buy?

5. Gemma had three packs of 12 felt tip pens and two packs of 25. How many felt tip pens did she have altogether?

6. Steven's book has 146 pages. He needs to read 25 more pages to reach half way. What page is he on?

7. England scored 314 runs in the first innings and 87 runs less in their second innings. How many runs did they score altogether?

8. How many hours are there in 4 weeks?

9. Mr. and Mrs. French went shopping. Mrs. French spent twice as much as her husband. Altogether they spent £78. How much did Mr. French spend?

10. A sweet shop had 100 ice lollies. One quarter were sold on Monday. One third of those left were sold on Tuesday. How many lollies were left?

On this page you will learn:

- to change pounds to pence and vice versa.

Example   365p = £3·65   72p = £0·72

- to solve problems using all four operations.

JOE'S CAFE – MENU

Sandwiches	£2·25	Tea per pot	88p
Rolls	£1·35	Coffee	99p
Pizza	£1·90	Coke	70p
Burger	£1·50	Milkshake	£1·30
Hot dog	£1·40	Hot Chocolate	£1·20
Chips	80p	Orange Squash	50p
Biscuits	45p	Blackcurrant	75p
Cakes	80p to £1·20	Ice cream	85p

French Fries

A

Change to pence.

1 £2·17   **3** £7·60

2 £4·28   **4** £9·43

Change to pounds and pence.

5 179p   **7** 68p

6 356p   **8** 892p

Use the menu. Work out the cost of each order.

9 5 cokes

10 burger and chips

11 sandwich and coffee

12 milkshake and biscuits

13 10 packets of biscuits

14 hot dog and ice cream

15 How many orange squashes could you buy for £5·00?

16 How much did each cake cost if you bought 5 cakes for £5·50?

Work out the change.

	Cost	Payment	Change
17	70p	£1·00	?
18	£3·50	£5·00	?
19	£6·20	£10·00	?
20	£2·80	£5·00	?
21	£4·10	£5·00	?
22	£8·30	£10·00	?

Make these amounts with the fewest possible coins.

23 43p		**29** 29p	
24 58p		**30** £1·07	
25 85p		**31** £3·90	
26 37p		**32** 74p	
27 £2·60		**33** 92p	
28 66p		**34** £4·35	

B

Change to pence.

1. £8·30
2. £4·28
3. £13·51
4. £11·07

Change to pounds and pence.

5. 637p
6. 506p
7. 830p
8. 1141p

Use the menu. Work out the cost of each order and the change from £10·00.

9. sandwich and tea
10. 4 hot chocolates
11. 10 ice creams
12. hot dog, ice cream and milkshake
13. 2 pizzas and a coke
14. 2 coffees and 2 biscuits

15. How many burgers could you buy for £10·00?

16. How much did each cake cost if you bought 5 cakes for £4·50?

17. You pay for a hot dog, chips and a drink with a £5·00 note.
    You receive £1·60 change. What was the drink?

18. You pay for a burger, a hot dog and a cake with a £5·00 note.
    You receive £1·15 change. How much did the cake cost?

C

Change to pence.

1. £16·42
2. 40·98
3. £31·05
4. £17·00

Change to pounds and pence.

5. 909p
6. 2083p
7. 3807p
8. 10 016p

Use the menu. Work out the total cost of each order and the change from £20·00.

9. 3 pizzas
   3 chips
   3 ice creams

10. 4 coffees
    2 biscuits
    3 hot chocolates

11. 5 sandwiches
    2 teas
    3 cokes

12. 10 rolls
    5 cokes
    1 coffee

13. 12 blackcurrants
    6 ice creams
    2 milkshakes

14. 8 burgers
    2 hot dogs
    6 chips

15. How many ice creams could you buy for £20·00?

16. How much did each cake cost if you bought 8 cakes for £7·60?

17. You pay for a sandwich, an ice cream and a drink with a £5·00 note.
    You receive £1·20 change. What was the drink?

18. You pay for 3 coffees and 3 identical cakes with a £10·00 note.
    You receive £4·48 change.
    How much did each cake cost?

COFFEE BREAK

On this page you will learn:

- **to use the relationship between metric units of length.**

$10\text{ mm} = 1\text{ cm}$
$5\text{ mm} = \frac{1}{2}\text{ cm}$
$1\text{ mm} = \frac{1}{10}\text{ cm}$

$100\text{ cm} = 1\text{ m}$
$50\text{ cm} = \frac{1}{2}\text{ m}$
$25\text{ cm} = \frac{1}{4}\text{ m}$
$10\text{ cm} = \frac{1}{10}\text{ m}$

$1000\text{ m} = 1\text{ km}$
$500\text{ m} = \frac{1}{2}\text{ km}$
$250\text{ m} = \frac{1}{4}\text{ km}$
$100\text{ m} = \frac{1}{10}\text{ km}$

Examples

$\frac{3}{4}\text{ m} = \square\text{ cm}$ Answer   75 cm

$1\frac{1}{2}\text{ km} = \square\text{ m}$ Answer   1500 m

$\frac{7}{10}\text{ m} = \square\text{ cm}$ Answer   70 cm

- **to suggest suitable units to measure lengths.**

If the length is less than 1 cm use millimetres.

If the length is less than 1 m use centimetres.

If the length is less than 1 km use metres.

A

Copy and complete by writing the missing number in the box.

1 $\frac{1}{2}\text{ km} = \square\text{ m}$ **7** $\frac{1}{2}\text{ m} = \square\text{ cm}$

2 $3\text{ km} = \square\text{ m}$ **8** $2\text{ m} = \square\text{ cm}$

3 $2\text{ km} = \square\text{ m}$ **9** $6\text{ m} = \square\text{ cm}$

4 $5000\text{ m} = \square\text{ km}$ **10** $400\text{ cm} = \square\text{ m}$

5 $3500\text{ m} = \square\text{ km}$ **11** $350\text{ cm} = \square\text{ m}$

6 $4500\text{ m} = \square\text{ km}$ **12** $800\text{ cm} = \square\text{ m}$

Suggest a suitable metric unit to measure these lengths.

13 a finger

14 the height of a tree

15 the length of England

16 a toothbrush

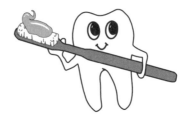

17 the length of the classroom

18 an apple pip

Think of two more things you would measure using:

19 centimetres

20 metres.

Choose the longest length from each pair.

21 500 m   5 km   **24** $\frac{1}{2}$ km   400 m

22 20 cm $\frac{1}{2}$ m   **25** 200 cm   1 m

23 40 cm $\frac{1}{4}$ m   **26** 400 m   4 km

B

Copy and complete by writing the missing number in the box.

1. $1\frac{1}{2}$ km $=\Box$ m
7. $\frac{3}{10}$ m $=\Box$ cm

2. $\frac{1}{4}$ km $=\Box$ m
8. $3\frac{6}{10}$ m $=\Box$ cm

3. $2\frac{3}{4}$ km $=\Box$ m
9. $\frac{1}{2}$ cm $=\Box$ mm

4. $1\frac{1}{10}$ km $=\Box$ m
10. $\frac{1}{10}$ cm $=\Box$ mm

5. $\frac{3}{4}$ m $=\Box$ cm
11. $\frac{7}{10}$ cm $=\Box$ mm

6. $2\frac{1}{2}$ m $=\Box$ cm
12. $2\frac{9}{10}$ cm $=\Box$ mm

Suggest a suitable metric unit to measure these lengths.

13. the height of a house

14. a smartie

15. the height of a book

16. the length of a playground

17. a motorway

18. a bottle

Think of two more things you would measure using:

19. millimetres

20. centimetres

21. metres

22. kilometres.

Copy and complete by writing >, < or = in the box.

23. $\frac{1}{10}$ cm $\Box$ 10 mm

24. $\frac{1}{2}$ km $\Box$ 120 m

25. 900 m $\Box$ 9 km

26. 6 mm $\Box$ $\frac{1}{2}$ cm

27. $\frac{3}{10}$ m $\Box$ 30 cm

28. 40 cm $\Box$ $\frac{1}{4}$ m

C

Copy and complete the tables.

1.

mm	cm
3 →	$\frac{3}{10}$
18 →	
→	$\frac{9}{10}$
→	$14\frac{7}{10}$

3.

m	km
720 →	$\frac{72}{100}$
4600 →	
→	$3\frac{1}{2}$
→	$2\frac{79}{100}$

2.

cm	m
290 →	$2\frac{9}{10}$
84 →	
→	$1\frac{3}{4}$
→	$4\frac{6}{100}$

4.

m	cm
$\frac{37}{100}$ →	
$1\frac{9}{10}$ →	
→	302
→	145

Copy and complete by choosing the most likely length.

5. A counter is (1 mm, 10 mm, 10 cm) wide.

6. A garden is (3 km, 300 m, 3000 cm) in length.

7. Jake walked (4 km, 40 km, 400 m) in one hour.

8. The stool is (5 cm, 50 cm, 500 cm) tall.

9. The match is (50 mm, 50 cm, 5 mm) long.

10. A dinosaur is about (2 m, 20 m, 2 km) long.

Arrange these lengths in order.
Start with the shortest.

11. 6 cm   26 mm $\frac{6}{10}$ cm $\frac{2}{10}$ m

12. 70 m $\frac{7}{10}$ km   7000 m   700 cm

13. $\frac{4}{100}$ km   44 m   4000 mm   400 m

14. 13 m $\frac{3}{100}$ km $\frac{3}{10}$ m   31 cm

On this page you will learn to solve problems involving length.

A

1 A snail crawls 45 cm. It crawls a further 26 cm.
How far has the snail crawled altogether?

2 A fence is 62 m long. 14 m is blown down.
How much of the fence is left standing?

3 How many 5 cm lengths of string can be cut from 40 cm?

4 Alan has four lengths of railway track, each 20 cm long.
How long is the track when he puts them together?

5 A rocket flies 230 m into the sky. A second rocket reaches 150 m higher.
How high does the second rocket fly?

B

1 Ross is 87 cm tall. Dee is 57 cm taller.
How tall is Dee in metres and centimetres?

2 A piece of guttering is 4 m long. A plumber cuts off 80 cm.
How long is the guttering now?

3 There are 20 magazines in a pile. Each magazine is 5 mm thick.
How high is the pile in centimetres?

4 Amy saws six lengths of wood. Each length is 25 cm.
What is the total length of the six pieces in metres.

5 Joe has a set of 30 encyclopaedias. He needs 1·2 m of shelving to store them.
How wide is each encyclopaedia?

C

1 A cyclist travels 300 m in one minute.
How many kilometres does he travel in 20 minutes?

2 The top shelf is one and a half metres long.
The bottom shelf is 64 cm shorter. How long is the bottom shelf?

3 2 m of ribbon is cut into eight equal lengths.
How long is each piece of ribbon?

4 58 cm is sawn off a piece of wood. 47 cm is left.
How long was the piece of wood before it was sawn?

5 At 8 o'clock in the morning a shadow was 1·4 m long.
At midday it was 87 cm shorter.
How long was the shadow at midday?

On this page you will learn to read scales accurately.

For each of the scales work out:
a) the measurement indicated by each of the arrows.
b) the difference between the two arrows.

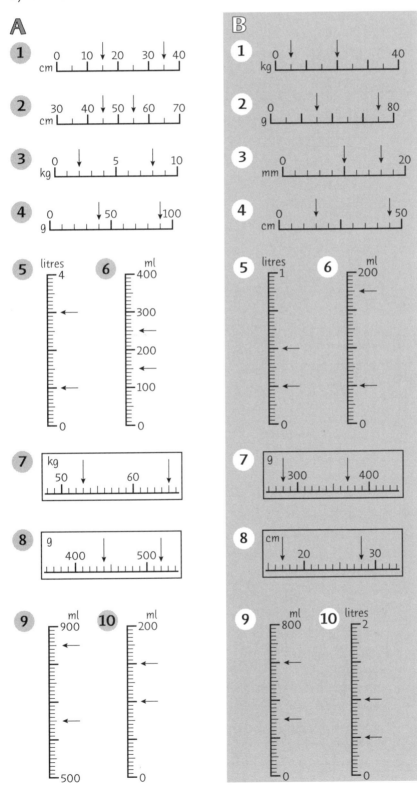

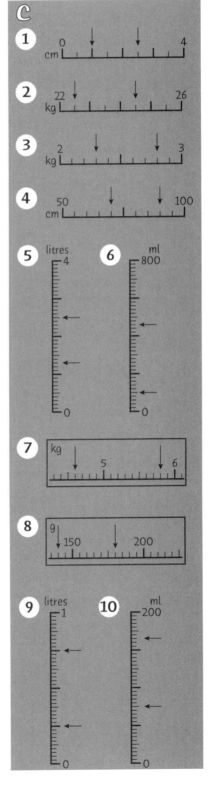

On this page you will learn to use the metric measures of mass.

1000 grams = 1 kilogram $500\,g = \frac{1}{2}\,kg$ $250\,g = \frac{1}{4}\,kg$ $750\,g = \frac{3}{4}\,kg$

$100\,g = \frac{1}{10}\,kg$ $200\,g = \frac{2}{10}\,kg$ $300\,g = \frac{3}{10}\,kg$ and so on

A

Copy and complete by writing the missing number in the box.

1 $1\,kg = \square\,g$

2 $2\,kg = \square\,g$

3 $1000\,g = \square\,kg$

4 $2500\,g = \square\,kg$

5 $\frac{1}{2}\,kg = \square\,g$

6 $2\frac{1}{2}\,kg = \square\,g$

7 $4000\,g = \square\,kg$

8 $1500\,g = \square\,kg$

9 $3\,kg = \square\,g$

10 $6\frac{1}{2}\,kg = \square\,g$

11 $5000\,g = \square\,kg$

12 $4500\,g = \square\,kg$

Would you use grams or kilograms to measure the mass of:

13 a feather

14 a sack of potatoes.

15 a watch

16 a lion?

B

Copy and complete by writing the missing number in the box.

1 $2\,kg = \square\,g$

2 $1\frac{1}{2}\,kg = \square\,g$

3 $250\,g = \square\,kg$

4 $1750\,g = \square\,kg$

5 $\frac{3}{4}\,kg = \square\,g$

6 $1\frac{7}{10}\,kg = \square\,g$

7 $3200\,g = \square\,kg$·

8 $4500\,g = \square\,kg$

9 $3\frac{1}{4}\,kg = \square\,g$

10 $\frac{9}{10}\,kg = \square\,g$

11 $6800\,g = \square\,kg$

12 $9250\,g = \square\,kg$

Would you use grams or kilograms to measure the mass of:

13 a teacher

14 a newspaper

15 a pavement slab

16 a bar of soap?

C

Copy and complete the tables.

1

g	kg
3000	→ 3
2750	→
1560	→
→	$2\frac{1}{4}$
→	$3\frac{1}{10}$
→	$1\frac{82}{100}$

2

kg	g
$5\frac{2}{10}$	→ 5200
	→ 1250
	→ 2480
$2\frac{3}{10}$	→
$4\frac{3}{4}$	→
$5\frac{17}{100}$	→

Copy and complete each sentence by choosing the best estimate.

3 An apple has a mass of (15 g, 150 g, 1500 g).

4 A box of cornflakes has a mass of ($\frac{3}{4}\,kg$, 3 kg, 34 kg).

5 A counter has a mass of about (1 g, 10 g, 100 g).

6 A mug has a mass of about (4 g, 40 g, 400 g).

On this page you will learn to solve problems involving mass.

A

1. A sack of potatoes weighs 56 kg. 24 kg are eaten.
   How much is left?
2. A coin weighs 20 g. How much do eight coins weigh?
3. Floyd weighs 45 kg. Carl weighs 32 kg more.
   How much does Carl weigh?
4. A cake weighs 800 g. It is cut into four slices.
   How much does each slice weigh?
5. There is 430 g of sugar in a bowl. 70 g is used.
   How much sugar is left?

B

1. A cake weighs one kilogram. It is cut into four slices.
   What does one slice weigh in grams?
2. The chocolates in a box all weigh 25 g.
   How many chocolates are there in a half kilogram box?
3. A can of beans weighs 400 g.
   How much do six cans weigh in kilograms?
4. A parcel weighs half a kilogram. Another weighs 300 g.
   What do they weigh together?
5. A newspaper weighs 200 g. A papergirl delivers 40 copies.
   What is the weight of the newspapers she carries in kilograms?

C

1. Jack weighed four and a half kilograms at birth. Jessica weighed 750 g less.
   What was Jessica's weight?
2. A serving of breakfast cereal weighs 30 g.
   How many servings are there in a three quarter kilogram box?
3. A crate of apples weighs four kilograms.
   If the crate weighs 200 g, how much do the apples weigh?
4. To make four loaves a baker uses half a kilogram of
   wholemeal flour and 800 g of plain flour.
   How much flour does he use altogether?
5. Dad's fish weighed 250 g.
   Jimmy's fish weighed twelve times as much.
   How much did Jimmy's fish weigh in kilograms?

On this page you will learn to use the metric measures of capacity.

1000 millilitres = 1 litre   500 ml = $\frac{1}{2}$ litre   250 ml = $\frac{1}{4}$ litre   750 ml = $\frac{3}{4}$ litre

100 ml = $\frac{1}{10}$ litre   200 ml = $\frac{2}{10}$ litre   300ml = $\frac{3}{10}$ litre and so on.

A

Copy and complete by writing the missing number in the box.

1. 1 litre = ☐ ml
2. 2 litres = ☐ ml
3. 1000 ml = ☐ litre
4. 1500 ml = ☐ litres
5. $\frac{1}{2}$ litre = ☐ ml
6. $2\frac{1}{2}$ litres = ☐ ml
7. 3000 ml = ☐ litres
8. 3500 ml = ☐ litres
9. $5\frac{1}{2}$ litres = ☐ ml
10. 7 litres = ☐ ml
11. 6000 ml = ☐ litres
12. 4500 ml = ☐ litres

Would you use litres or millilitres to measure:

13. a bottle of soap bubbles
14. a swimming pool
15. a lake
16. a raindrop?

B

Copy and complete by writing the missing number in the box.

1. $1\frac{1}{2}$ litres = ☐ ml
2. $\frac{1}{4}$ litre = ☐ ml
3. 2000 ml = ☐ litres
4. 1250 ml = ☐ litres
5. $1\frac{3}{4}$ litres = ☐ ml
6. $3\frac{7}{10}$ litres = ☐ ml
7. 2500 ml = ☐ litres
8. 600 ml = ☐ litres
9. $2\frac{1}{4}$ litres = ☐ ml
10. $\frac{3}{10}$ litre = ☐ ml
11. 4750 ml = ☐ litres
12. 9100 ml = ☐ litres

Would you use litres or millilitres to measure:

13. a bucket
14. a wine glass
15. a water pistol
16. a bath?

C

Copy and complete the tables.

1.

ml	litres
5000 →	5
1200 →	
3500 →	
→	2
→	$\frac{3}{4}$
→	$2\frac{1}{4}$

2.

litres	ml
$1\frac{8}{10}$ →	1800
$4\frac{1}{2}$ →	
$1\frac{3}{10}$ →	
→	2750
→	250
→	900

Copy and complete each sentence by choosing the best estimate.

3. The capacity of a washing up bowl is (50 ml, 500 ml, 5000 ml).
4. A perfume bottle contains (2 ml, 20 ml, 200 ml).
5. A small sachet contains (3 ml, 30 ml, 300 ml) of shampoo.
6. A paddling pool has a capacity of (300 ml, 3000 ml, 3000 l).

On this page you will learn to solve problems involving capacity.

A

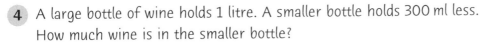

1 80 buckets of water fill a pond. Each bucket holds 2 litres.
How much water does the pond hold?

2 There is 500 ml of lemonade in a bottle.
Joanne pours out 200 ml.
How much lemonade is there now in the bottle?

3 Philip takes two spoonfuls of medicine every day.
Each spoonful is 5 ml.
How much medicine does he take in seven days?

4 A large bottle of wine holds 1 litre. A smaller bottle holds 300 ml less.
How much wine is in the smaller bottle?

5 A glass of orange squash is made with 30 ml of orange and 230 ml of water.
How much orange squash is there?

B

1 An ice cream tub holds two litres. 500 ml is used.
How much ice cream is left in the tub?

2 Six 150 ml cups are filled from a jug holding one litre of water.
How much water is left?

3 A mug of tea holds one quarter of a litre.
How many mugs can be filled from a 5 litre urn?

4 Jordan mixes 700 ml of red paint with two and a half litres of white paint.
How much pink paint has he made?

5 Half of a one litre carton of milk is used. Louise pours out a further 150 ml.
How much milk is left in the carton?

C

1 How many 150 ml glasses can be filled from one and a half litres?

2 There are one and three quarter litres of water in a bowl.
400 ml is added. How much water is there now in the bowl?

3 20 cartons of milk are delivered. Each carton holds 200 ml.
How much milk is delivered in litres?

4 A saucepan holds 2 litres of boiling water. One tenth of the
water evaporates. How much water is left in the saucepan?

5 A glass contains one quarter of a litre of orange squash.
175 ml of water was used in making the drink. How much squash was used?

On these pages you will learn:

- **to calculate the areas of shapes by counting squares.**

  The area of a shape is the amount of surface it covers.
  Area is measured in squares, usually square centimetres (cm^2) or square metres (m^2).

- **to measure and calculate the perimeter of a shape.**

  The perimeter of a shape is the distance around its edges.
  The perimeter of a field is the fence around it. The area is the field itself.

  Example   Area of rectangle $= 24\,cm^2$

                       Perimeter $= 6\,cm + 4\,cm + 6\,cm + 4\,cm$
                                  $= 20\,cm$

A

Measure each shape and work out the perimeter.

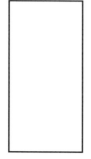      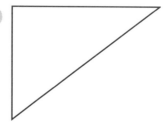

Use squared paper. Draw the following shapes and find:
a) the area of each shape.   b) the perimeter of each shape.

④ A rectangle with sides of 5 cm and 4 cm.

⑤ A square with sides of 6 cm.

⑥ A rectangle with side of 8 cm and 3 cm.

⑦ A square with sides of 8 cm.

⑧ Draw a square with an area of $16\,cm^2$. Work out the perimeter.

⑨ Draw a rectangle with a length of 6 cm and a perimeter of 20 cm. Work out the area.

⑩ Draw a rectangle with an area of $15\,cm^2$ and a length of 5 cm. Work out the perimeter.

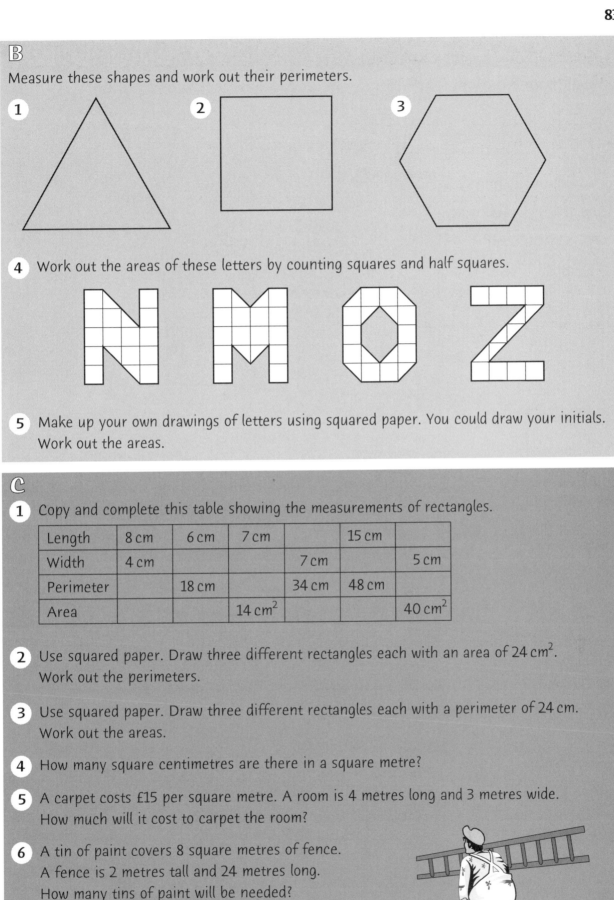

B

Measure these shapes and work out their perimeters.

1   2   3

4   Work out the areas of these letters by counting squares and half squares.

N M O Z

5   Make up your own drawings of letters using squared paper. You could draw your initials. Work out the areas.

C

1   Copy and complete this table showing the measurements of rectangles.

Length	8 cm	6 cm	7 cm		15 cm	
Width	4 cm			7 cm		5 cm
Perimeter		18 cm		34 cm	48 cm	
Area			14 cm²			40 cm²

2   Use squared paper. Draw three different rectangles each with an area of 24 cm². Work out the perimeters.

3   Use squared paper. Draw three different rectangles each with a perimeter of 24 cm. Work out the areas.

4   How many square centimetres are there in a square metre?

5   A carpet costs £15 per square metre. A room is 4 metres long and 3 metres wide. How much will it cost to carpet the room?

6   A tin of paint covers 8 square metres of fence. A fence is 2 metres tall and 24 metres long. How many tins of paint will be needed?

On this page you will learn to use the vocabulary related to time.

You should know and be able to use these facts and this rhyme.

1 millennium	= 1000 years
1 century	= 100 years
1 year	= 12 months
	= 52 weeks
1 week	= 7 days
1 day	= 24 hours
1 hour	= 60 minutes
1 minute	= 60 seconds

30 days has September,
April, June and November.
All the rest have 31,
Save for February alone,
Which has but 28 days clear
And 29 in each leap year.

Leap years come every 4 years. 2000 was a leap year.

A

Write as minutes.

1. 5 hours
2. $1\frac{1}{2}$ hours
3. 120 seconds
4. 30 seconds

Write as days.

5. 2 weeks
6. 5 weeks
7. 48 hours
8. 240 hours

Write as years.

9. 365 days
10. $\frac{1}{2}$ century
11. 24 months
12. 104 weeks

13. The 12 months of the year are listed here in alphabetical order.

April	February	June	November
August	January	March	October
December	July	May	September

Month	Days
January	31
February	28 or 29

Copy and complete the table by writing all
12 months in the correct order.

Look at the calendar.

14. How many days are there in December?

15. On which day of the week falls:
    a) December 1st?
    b) December 31st?

16. How many Fridays are there in the month?

17. What is the date of the second Tuesday in the month?

18. On which day does Christmas Day fall?

DECEMBER						
Su	M	Tu	W	Th	F	Sa
			1	2	3	4
5	6	7	8	9	10	11
12	13	14	15	16	17	18
19	20	21	22	23	24	25
26	27	28	29	30	31	

B

Write as minutes.

1 8 hours
2 $2\frac{1}{4}$ hours
3 240 seconds
4 90 seconds

Write as days.

5 4 weeks
6 6 weeks
7 36 hours
8 120 hours

Write as years.

9 6 decades
10 2 centuries
11 36 months
12 18 months

How many days are there in:

13 May
14 September

15 February 2004
16 April and May

17 June and July
18 December and January?

19 My birthday is on the last day in November. Today is the 7th November.
How many days do I have to wait for my birthday?

20 Today is September 5th. Jade is 9 days old.
On what day was she born?

C

Write as minutes.

1 9 hours
2 $2\frac{3}{4}$ hours
3 480 seconds
4 135 seconds

Write as weeks.

5 $\frac{1}{2}$ year
6 4 years
7 42 days
8 1 century

Write as years.

9 48 months
10 78 weeks
11 15 decades
12 $\frac{1}{2}$ millenium

Look at the calendar.
On what day will these children have their birthdays?

13 Kerry   September 6th
14 Jamie   September 18th
15 Zoe   August 29th
16 Ryan   October 10th

17 The new school year begins on the first Monday in September. Give the date.

18 The first half term lasts for seven weeks.
On what date does the half term end?

19 Write out the calendar for August.

SEPTEMBER						
Su	M	Tu	W	Th	F	Sa
			1	2	3	4
5	6	7	8	9	10	11
12	13	14	15	16	17	18
19	20	21	22	23	24	25
26	27	28	29	30		

On these pages you will learn to read the time to the nearest minute.

Analogue clocks have faces. Read the minutes as:
'past' before 30minutes.
'to' after 30 minutes.

a.m. means before 12 noon

Examples

morning
22 minutes past 8
8 : 22 a.m.

Digital clocks have figures only.
The minutes are always shown as
minutes past the hour.

p.m. means after 12 noon

Examples

evening
12 minutes to 7
6 : 48 p.m.

A

Write each time shown:
a) in words   b) in figures, using a.m. or p.m..

1 morning

2 evening

3 night

4 afternoon

5 afternoon

6 breakfast

7 bedtime

8 night

9 morning

10 afternoon

11 night

12 playtime

B

Write each time shown to the nearest minute:

a) in words   b) in figures, using a.m. or p.m..

1 morning

2 afternoon

3 night

4 morning

5 morning

6 bedtime

7 morning

8 evening

9 Write the times in figures, using a.m. or p.m., if each of the eight clocks above was 25 minutes fast?

10 Write the times in figures, using a.m. or p.m., if each of the eight clocks above was 4 hours slow?

C

1 Copy and complete the table.

TIME IN WORDS	12-HOUR CLOCK	24-HOUR CLOCK
half past eight	8:30 p.m.	20:30
		07:06
		11:47
		21:54
		04:25
	3:43 p.m.	
	8:09 a.m.	
	1:11 p.m.	
	1:28 a.m.	
	4:32 p.m.	

2 What would each 24 hour clock time be if the clocks in the table were:
a) 16 minutes slow   b) 40 minutes fast?

3 How many hours and minutes are there between each pair of times?
a) 8:30 a.m. and 13:00   c) 22:15 and 2:05 a.m.
b) 2:30 a.m. and 12:25   d) 11:35 and 4:15 p.m.

On this page you will learn to use timetables.

	BBC1		ITV
2:15	Tennis	3:10	Carry on Nurse (Film)
4:45	Doctor Who (Drama)	4:55	Home and Away (Soap)
5:10	Newsround	5:20	Wheel of Fortune (Game Show)
5:20	Blue Peter	5:50	National News
5:45	Local News	6:28	Weather
6:00	National News	6:30	Local News
6:30	Weather	6:50	Wish You Were Here
6:35	Sports Quiz (Game Show)	7:15	Coronation Street (Soap)
6:55	Gardener's World	7:45	Football
7:30	Eastenders (Soap)	9:40	National News
8:00	Casualty (Drama)	10:00	The Bill (Drama)
8:45	Points of View	11:15	The South Bank Show

A

Use the timetable of television programmes.
How long are the following programmes?

1 Newsround

2 Blue Peter

3 Wheel of Fortune

4 Coronation Street

Which programme could you watch on BBC1 at these times?

5 6:00   **6** 8:45   **7** 7:00   **8** 3:30

Which two programmes could you watch at each of these times?

9 5:20   **10** 6:30   **11** 4:00   **12** 7:30

13 The journey from the Station to the Hospital takes 20 minutes.
Buses run every 15 minutes.
Copy and complete the times on this bus timetable.

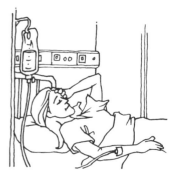

	Bus 1	Bus 2	Bus 3	Bus 4	Bus 5	Bus 6
Station	9:00	9:15				
Hospital	9:20					

14 Which bus would a nurse need to be on if she started work at:

a) 9:30

b) 10:30

c) 10:15

d) 10:45?

B

Use the timetable of television programmes.
How long are the following programmes?

1 Doctor Who   **4** Wish You Were Here

2 Sports Quiz   **5** Tennis

3 The Bill   **6** Carry on Nurse

Which two programmes could you watch at each of these times?

7 5:00   **8** 5:30   **9** 6:40   **10** 7:20

11 The journey from the Village to the Superstore takes 35 minutes.
Buses run every 20 minutes.
Copy and complete the times on this bus timetable.

	Bus 1	Bus 2	Bus 3	Bus 4	Bus 5	Bus 6
Village	9:15					
Superstore	9:50					

C

Use the timetable of television programmes.
What is the total length of the following types of programmes?

1 Game Shows   **3** Local News   **5** Drama

2 Soaps   **4** National News   **6** Sports

If you watched the following programmes to the end and then changed channels, which programme would you be watching?

7 Doctor Who   **9** Wish You Were Here   **11** Coronation Street

8 Sports Quiz   **10** Tennis   **12** Wheel of Fortune

13 Copy and complete this train timetable.
Each train takes the same time between stations.

	Train 1	Train 2	Train 3	Train 4	Train 5	Train 6
Oldport	8:00	8:47	9:23	9:56	10:34	11:09
Highcliff	8:06					
Whitehill	8:19			10:15		
Westham	8:38					
City Centre	8:45		10:08			

On this page you will solve problems involving time.

A

1. A car race started at 2:20. It finished at 3:00.
   How long did the race last?

2. Andy set off for school at 8:10.
   His journey took 35 minutes.
   At what time did he arrive at school?

3. Ann's favourite programme lasts for 30 minutes.
   It finishes at 7:50. At what time does it start?

4. Playtime lasts for 20 minutes. It starts at 10:25.
   At what time does it end?

5. A cake needs to be baked for 40 minutes. Wendy puts the cake in the oven at 3:30.
   When does she take it out?

B

1. Joan starts writing her story at 9:17. The lesson finishes at 10:00.
   How long is she writing?

2. The film starts at 6:30. It lasts for 80 minutes.
   At what time does it end?

3. Football practice lasts for 45 minutes. It finishes at 4:20.
   At what time does it start?

4. Peter arrived home at 3:50. He spent 30 minutes doing his homework and 20 minutes
   having tea. At what time did he sit down to watch television?

5. Dilip puts on a CD at 2:15. It lasts for 55 minutes. When does it finish?

C

1. The game of cricket begins at 11:20. It finishes at 16:55.
   How long does it last?

2. David falls asleep at 22:30. He sleeps for 8 hours.
   At what time does he wake up?

3. A coach leaves London at 10:45.
   It arrives in Sheffield at 14:25.
   How long does the journey take?

4. The fete lasts 3 hours 20 minutes. It finishes at 17:15.
   When did the fete begin?

5. The school day lasts 6 hours and 25 minutes.
   It begins at 08:50. When is hometime?

On this page you will learn to construct 2-D shapes and discuss their properties.

In the following problems you will be making different shapes on a 3 × 3 grid. Each shape should be different.

These quadrilaterals are the same. Make sure that all of your shapes are different.

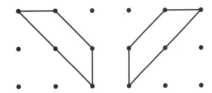

 A

1 Use a pinboard, squared paper or dotty paper. Make different quadrilaterals on a 3 × 3 grid. Record them on squared paper or dotty paper.

Examples

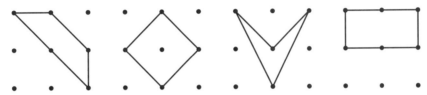

2 Which of your quadrilaterals are squares or rectangles?

3 Which of your quadrilaterals are symmetrical?

B

1 Use a pinboard, squared paper or dotty paper.
Make different pentagons on a 3 × 3 grid.
Record them on squared paper or dotty paper.

Examples

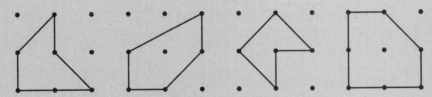

2 Which of your pentagons are symmetrical?

3 Which of your pentagons are convex and which are concave?

C

1 Use squared or dotty paper.
Make different hexagons on a 3 × 3 grid.

Example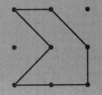

2 If your hexagon is symmetrical draw on the line of symmetry.

3 How many convex hexagons is it possible to make?

On these pages you will learn to classify 2-D shapes.

2-D shapes with straight lines are called polygons.
(Equal lines are shown with dashes and equal angles are marked.)

A three-sided polygon is a *triangle*.

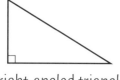
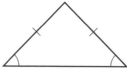
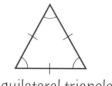

right-angled triangle · isosceles triangle · equilateral triangle

A four-sided polygon is a *quadrilateral*.

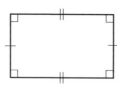

quadrilateral · oblong or rectangle · square

OTHER POLYGONS

5 sides – pentagon   7 sides – heptagon
6 sides – hexagon   8 sides – octagon

REGULAR POLYGONS

All sides and all angles
are equal.

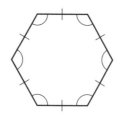

IRREGULAR POLYGONS

Sides and angles
are not all equal.

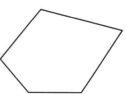

CONCAVE POLYGONS

One angle greater
than 180°.

CONVEX POLYGONS

No angle greater
than 180°.

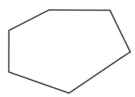

Here are some shapes.

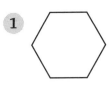   

 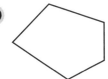

A

Copy and complete the table for each of the shapes.

Number	Number of sides	Name of polygon
1	6	hexagon

B

1 Write the name of each of the above shapes. (e.g. square, regular pentagon, etc.)

2 Which of the shapes are concave?

3 Draw a concave pentagon and a convex pentagon. Label them.

4 Draw a concave hexagon and a convex hexagon. Label them.

C

1 Copy and complete the table for all the shapes.

Number	Name of shape	Number of equal sides	Number of equal angles
1	regular hexagon	6	6

2 What is the common name for a regular quadrilateral?

3 What is the common name for a regular triangle?

4 Draw an isosceles triangle with one angle greater than 90°.

5 Draw a quadrilateral with 3 angles greater than 90°.

On these pages you will learn to classify 3-D shapes according to their properties.

SHAPES WITH CURVED FACES

These 3-D shapes have curved faces.

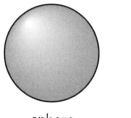  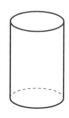 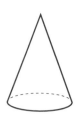

sphere   hemi-sphere   cylinder   cone

SHAPES WITH STRAIGHT EDGES

A 3-D shape with straight edges is called a *polyhedron.*

A regular polyhedron has faces which are identical.

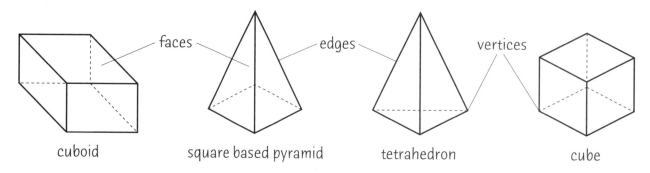

cuboid   square based pyramid   tetrahedron   cube

faces   edges   vertices

PRISMS

A prism is a polyhedron with two identical end faces and the same cross section throughout its length.

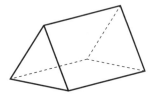 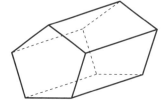 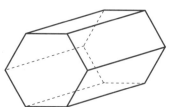

triangular based prism   pentagonal based prism   hexagonal based prism

Here are some shapes.

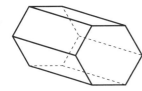

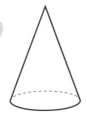

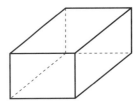

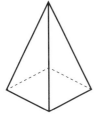

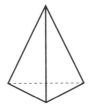

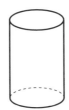

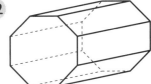

A

Think of things which look like each of the shapes.

B

1. Write down the name of each of the above shapes?

2. Which of the shapes have curved faces?

3. Which of the shapes are regular polyhedra (plural of polyhedron)?

4. Which of the shapes are prisms?

C

Copy and complete the table for each of the eight shapes with only flat faces.

No.	Shape	Flat Faces	Edges	Vertices
1	hexagonal prism	8	18	12

On this page you will learn to make nets for 3-D shapes.

A

1 Copy these nets onto squared paper.
Cut them out and fold them to make open cubes.

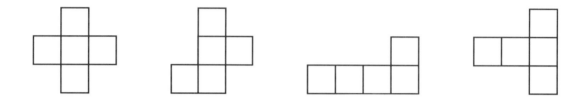

2 Can you find different nets that will make open cubes?

B

1 Copy these nets onto squared paper.
Cut them out and fold them to make closed cubes.

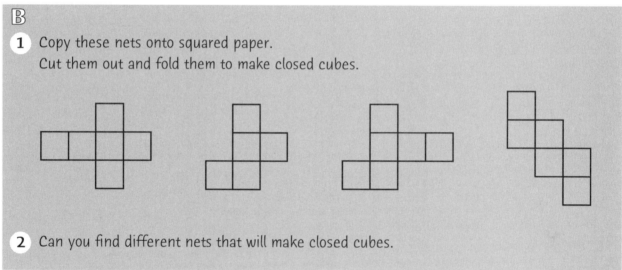

2 Can you find different nets that will make closed cubes.

C

1 Copy this net onto squared paper.
Cut it out and fold it to make a cuboid.

2 Make nets for these cuboids.
a)

b)

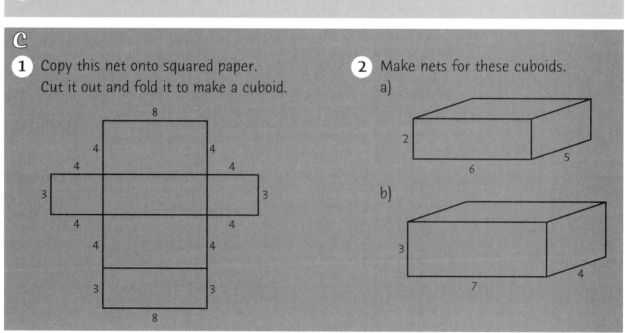

On this page you will learn to visualise 3-D shapes from 2-D drawings.

1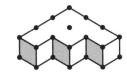

6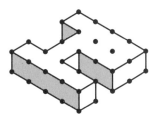

11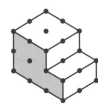

2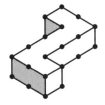

7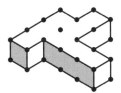

12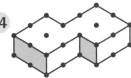

3

8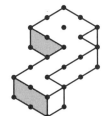

13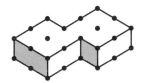

4

9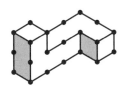

14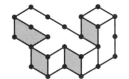

5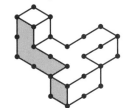

10

15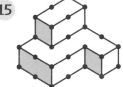

A

Use cubes to build these shapes.

B

Without using cubes, work out how many cubes are needed to build these shapes.

C

How many more cubes are needed to make each shape into a cuboid?

Examples

1 3 cubes are needed.

2 6 cubes are needed.

On this page you will learn to recognise reflective symmetry in 2-D shapes.

A shape is symmetrical if half of its shape matches the other half exactly.
The line separating the two halves is the line of symmetry or mirror line.

Examples

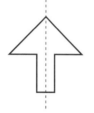

One line of symmetry

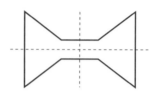

Two lines of symmetry

A

Which of the letters below have:

1 one line of symmetry?

2 two or more lines of symmetry?

3 no lines of symmetry?

Which of the shapes below have:

4 one line of symmetry?

5 two or more lines of symmetry?

6 no lines of symmetry?

B N W H D F
X M O K R Z

B

1 Look at the letters in Section A.
Copy the letters which are
symmetrical.
Draw on the line(s) of symmetry.

2 Look at the shapes in Section A.
Use squared paper. Draw the shapes
which are symmetrical.
Draw on the line(s) of symmetry.

C

Draw three shapes with:

1 one line of symmetry.

2 two lines of symmetry.

3 more than two lines of symmetry.

Example

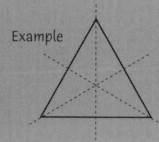

An equilateral
triangle has three
lines of symmetry

On this page you will learn to sketch the reflection of a simple shape in a mirror line.

Examples

Copy the shape and the mirror line and sketch the reflection.

A

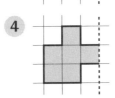

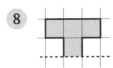

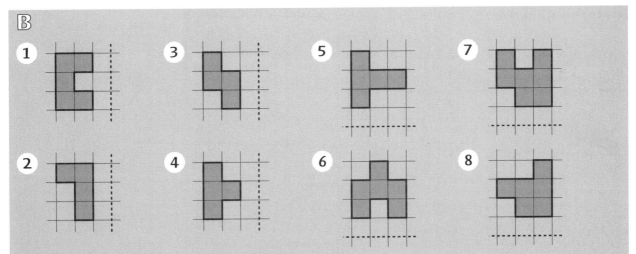

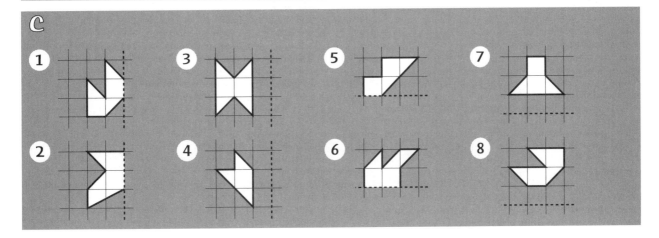

On this page you will learn to make patterns by repeatedly translating a shape.

Translating a shape means moving it in a straight line.

Example

Make a pattern by repeatedly translating a shape:

a) one square horizontally.   b) one square vertically.   c) half a square horizontally.

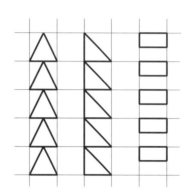
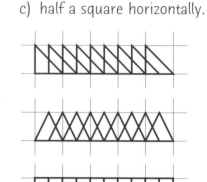

A

1 Use any of the shapes below or make up your own shapes.

Make a pattern by repeatedly translating shapes one square:

a) in a horizontal line.   b) in a vertical line.

B

1 Use any of the shapes above, or make up your own shape.

Repeatedly translate the shape in a horizontal line:

a) $\frac{1}{2}$ square   b) 2 squares   c) $1\frac{1}{2}$ squares.

2 Use the same shape. Do exactly the same but this time work vertically.

3 Make more patterns in the same way with different shapes.

C

1 The isosceles triangle is made in two squares.
Here it is repeatedly translated two squares.
Use the same shape but repeatedly translate it:
a) 1 square   b) $\frac{1}{2}$ square   c) $1\frac{1}{2}$ squares.

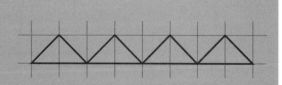

2 Investigate the patterns made by repeatedly translating other shapes made in two squares.

On a dartboard the outer ring doubles the score and the inner ring trebles the score. (Trebles means times by 3.)

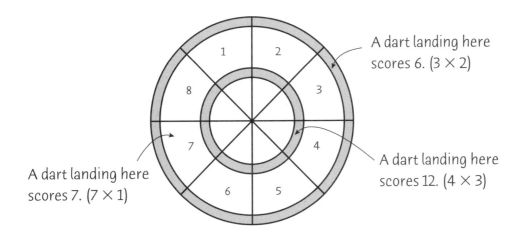

A dart landing here scores 6. (3 × 2)

A dart landing here scores 12. (4 × 3)

A dart landing here scores 7. (7 × 1)

A

Use one dart only in all the questions in this section.

1. What is the highest possible score?

2. Find two ways of scoring:
   a) 8   c) 4
   b) 2   d) 12.

3. Which number can be scored in three different ways?

4. Write down one way of scoring:
   a) 9   d) 10
   b) 14   e) 15
   c) 21   f) 16.

5. There are four numbers lower than 20 that you cannot score. What are they?

B

In this section use two darts only. Both darts must score.

1. What is the highest possible score with two darts?

2. Find two ways of scoring:
   a) 34   b) 39.

3. Find four ways of scoring:
   a) 36   c) 32
   b) 33   d) 29.

4. How can you score:
   a) 35   c) 38
   b) 37   d) 40?

5. Explore different ways of scoring these numbers.
   a) 17   b) 26   c) 31.

C

In this section use three darts only. All three darts must score.

1. What is the highest possible score using three darts?

2. How can you score 59?

3. There are three ways of scoring 58. What are they?

4. Which numbers in the 60s cannot be scored?

5. Explore different ways of scoring these numbers:
   a) 47 b) 51 c) 55.

6. Design a dartboard of your own. Investigate the scores that can be made on it, and the scores that cannot be made.

On this page you will learn to use co-ordinates to find the position of a point on a grid.

The position of a point on a grid is given by its co-ordinates.

Examples

The position of Point A.
Start at the origin, (0, 0).
Go across 4 and up 2.
Point A is (4, 2).

Point B is (2, 4).
Across 2 and up 4.

Remember: The across co-ordinate comes first.

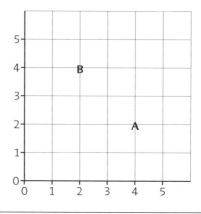

A

Use the grid to work out the message written in co-ordinates.
Each column spells out a word.

1.
(4, 1)	(2, 0)	(2, 3)	(1, 8)	(3, 6)
(2, 3)	(2, 7)	(8, 1)	(2, 7)	(6, 5)
(3, 2)	(6, 0)	(7, 3)	(2, 7)	(8, 1)
(7, 4)	(6, 8)		(7, 3)	

2.
(7 4)	(6, 2)	(7, 3)	(8, 5)	(2, 0)
(2, 7)	(2, 3)	(2, 7)	(6, 2)	(4, 1)
(6, 5)	(3, 7)	(8, 1)	(1, 5)	(4, 5)
	(4, 1)	(4, 1)	(3, 2)	(4, 5)

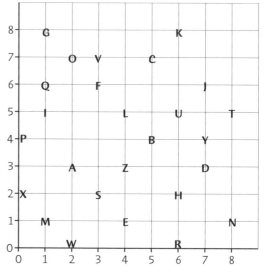

3. Draw a 5 × 5 grid like the one shown below. Plot the points. Join them up in the order given. Use a different colour for each shape. What shapes have you drawn?

A	B	C	D
(1, 2)	(1, 0)	(3, 1)	(0, 4)
(1, 5)	(2, 3)	(3, 4)	(2, 4)
(4, 5)	(3, 0)	(5, 4)	(0, 1)
(4, 2)	(1, 0)	(5, 1)	(0, 4)
(1, 2)		(3, 1)	

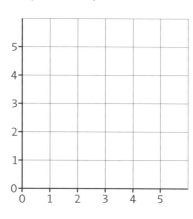

B

1 Use the grid to work out the message written in co-ordinates.
Each column spells out a word.

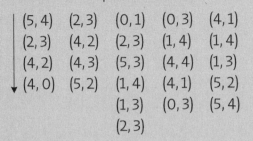

(5,4)	(2,3)	(0,1)	(0,3)	(4,1)
(2,3)	(4,2)	(2,3)	(1,4)	(1,4)
(4,2)	(4,3)	(5,3)	(4,4)	(1,3)
(4,0)	(5,2)	(1,4)	(4,1)	(5,2)
		(1,3)	(0,3)	(5,4)
		(2,3)		

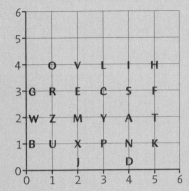

2

(0,2)	(3,2)	(4,1)	(3,4)	(5,2)
(1,3)	(1,4)	(4,2)	(4,4)	(5,4)
(4,4)	(1,1)	(2,2)	(5,1)	(4,4)
(5,2)	(1,3)	(2,3)	(2,3)	(4,3)
(2,3)				

3 Draw a 6 × 6 grid.
Plot the points in the first column.
Join them up in the order given.
You have drawn a letter.
Use a different colour for each letter.

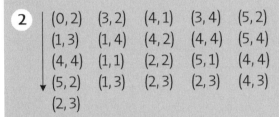

(1,0)	(2,2)	(3,0)	(0,4)
(1,5)	(2,6)	(3,4)	(1,0)
(3,3)	(4,5)	(6,0)	(2,2)
(5,5)	(2,4)	(6,4)	(3,0)
(0,5)	(4,2)		(4,4)

C

1 Use the grid above to work out the message written in co-ordinates.
Each column spells out a word.

(4,2)	(5,2)	(1,3)	(4,2)	(1,1)	(5,2)	(4,3)
(3,3)	(5,4)	(1,4)	(4,1)	(3,1)	(5,4)	(5,2)
(1,3)	(2,3)	(1,4)	(4,0)		(2,3)	(4,2)
(1,4)		(2,2)				(4,4)
(4,3)						(1,3)
(4,3)						(4,3)

2 Draw a 12 × 5 grid. (12 along the horizontal axis). Plot the co-ordinates, working across.
Join them up in the order given to make a picture.

(0,3) (3,3) (5,5) (9,5) (10,3) (12,3) (12,1) (11,1) (10,0)
(9,0) (8,1) (4,1) (3,0) (2,0) (1,1) (0,1) (0,3)

3 Make up your own grid picture and write down the co-ordinates.

4 Use the grid with letters in section A.
Write the following names in co-ordinates.
a) your name
b) a pop star
c) a teacher
d) a sportsman
Ask a friend to work out your names.

On this page you will learn to recognise horizontal, vertical and diagonal lines.

The horizon is in the far distance where the land meets the sky.

A horizontal line is a flat line drawn in the direction of the horizon.

A vertical line is at right angles to a horizontal line.

A diagonal line goes from one corner to another.

Examples

Horizontal lines – top and bottom of the flag.

Vertical lines – sides of the flag.

Diagonal lines – cross on the flag.

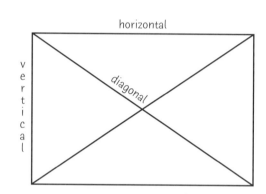

A

Use squared paper.

Copy each flag in a 6 × 4 grid.

Use one colour for all the horizontal lines of the flags.

Use a second colour for all the vertical lines of the flags.

Use a third colour for all the diagonal lines of the flags.

1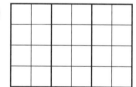

4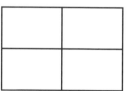

7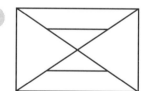

2

5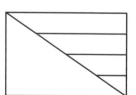

8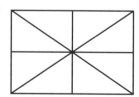

3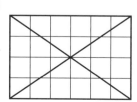

6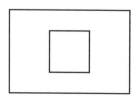

9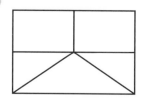

B

Use squared paper. Copy each flag in a 6 × 4 grid.

Use one colour for all the horizontal lines.

Use a second colour for all the vertical lines.

Use a third colour for all the diagonal lines or parts of diagonal lines.

Use a fourth colour for all the other lines.

1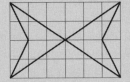

4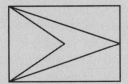

7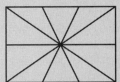

2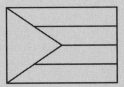

5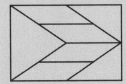

8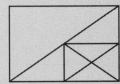

3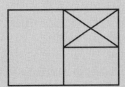

6

9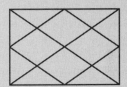

C

1 Use squared paper. Copy each letter in a 4 × 4 grid.

Use one colour for all the horizontal lines.

Use a second colour for all the vertical lines.

Use a third colour for all the diagonals or parts of diagonals of the 4 × 4 grid. (Not the diagonals of the small squares)

Use a fourth colour for all the other lines.

    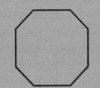

2 Now draw each of the ten numerals in a 4 × 4 grid. Use the same four colours to show the same types of lines.

On these pages you will learn to use compass directions.

Example

Start at X.
Go N   3 squares.
then SE   4 squares.
then W   7 squares.
You are at (2, 4).

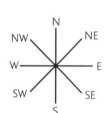

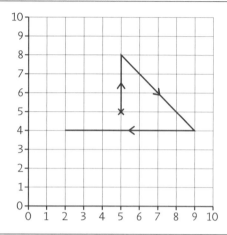

A

Start at X. Follow the directions.
Give the co-ordinates of the square at which you arrive.

1 S3 squares
E2 squares
N4 squares

3 E5 squares
N2 squares
W5 squares

5 N3 squares
E2 squares
S7 squares

7 W3 squares
N2 squares
E6 squares

2 N4 squares
W3 squares
S6 squares

4 W2 squares
S1 squares
E4 squares

6 S4 squares
W3 squares
N5 squares

8 E5 squares
N4 squares
W4 squares

9 Draw a grid like this.
Follow the instructions to draw a picture.
The first 4 lines are shown.

Start at (3, 1)

Go | N5 squares   S2 squares
W2 squares   W2 squares
N1 square   S5 squares
E7 squares   W1 squares
N2 squares   N3 squares
E1 square   W4 squares
S1 square   S3 squares
E2 squares   W1 squares

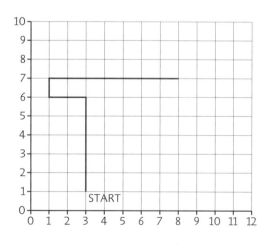

10 Look at the map on page 107.
Which town do you come to if you travel:
a) north from Dartley
b) south from Bigton
c) east from Farham
d) west from Dartley?

B

Use the grid on the opposite page. Start at X. Follow the directions.
Give the co-ordinates of the square at which you arrive.

1 SW5 squares
N3 squares
NE5 squares

3 SE4 squares
W2 squares
NW5 squares

5 N5 squares
SW3 squares
SE6 squares

7 NW2 squares
SW3 squares
SE3 squares

2 E3 squares
NW2 squares
S6 squares

4 NE4 squares
W3 squares
SW4 squares

6 S5 squares
NE3 squares
NW6 squares

8 W3 squares
NE4 squares
SE2 squares

9 In which direction would you travel going from:

a) Ashdean to Dartley
b) Bigton to Farham
c) Emford to Dartley
d) Charing to Dartley

e) Emford to Farham
f) Charing to Bigton
g) Garbury to Ashdean
h) Farham to Garbury?

C

Use the grid on the opposite page. Start at X. Follow the directions.
Give the co-ordinates of the square at which you arrive.

1 N4 squares
SW3 squares
SE5 squares
NE3 squares

3 E5 squares
NW4 squares
SW5 squares
E6 squares

5 S3 squares
NW5 squares
NE2 squares
SE6 squares

7 W5 squares
NE3 squares
SE7 squares
S1 squares

2 SW3 squares
N4 squares
NE2 squares
SE4 squares

4 NW4 squares
E7 squares
SE2 squares
SW5 squares

6 SE4 squares
W6 squares
NW3 squares
NE4 squares

8 NE3 squares
W4 squares
SW3 squares
SE4 squares

9 Draw a grid like the one at the top of page 106.
Follow the instructions to draw a picture.

Start at (0, 2)

Go				
E4 squares	E4 squares	E1 square	SW2 squares	SW2 squares
S2 squares	NW2 squares	NW2 squares	E1 square	E1 square
E2 squares	E1 square	E1 square	SW2 squares	SW2 squares
N2 squares	NW2 squares	NW2 squares	E1 square	

10 Start at any point on a 10 × 10 grid and give directions to draw a simple picture.
For example, you might choose to draw a boat, a car, a church, etc..

On these pages you will learn to make, measure and order angles.

An angle measures the amount something turns or rotates.
Angles are measured in degrees (°).

A whole turn is 360°.　　　A half turn is 180°.　　　A right angle is 90°.

The minute hand of
a clock turns:
360° in one hour.
180° in 30 minutes.
90° in 15 minutes.

Turning in a clockwise
direction from:
N to S is 180°.
N to E is 90°.
N to NE is 45°.

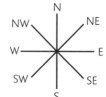

A

Use a set square to measure these angles. Decide if they are:
a) right angles.　　　b) greater than a right angle.　　　c) less than a right angle.

1   **3**   **5**   **7**

2   **4**   **6**   **8**

Find the new time if the hour hand turns these angles from:

12 o'clock	6 o'clock	3 o'clock	9 o'clock
9 180°	**12** 90°	**15** 180°	**18** 360°
10 90°	**13** 180°	**16** 360°	**19** 90°
11 360°	**14** 360°	**17** 90°	**20** 180°

How many degrees is the turn:

Clockwise

21 N to S   **23** S to W

22 W to S   **24** E to W?

How many degrees is the turn:

Anti-clockwise

25 E to N   **27** W to E

26 S to N   **28** N to E?

B

Use set squares to make angles of:

1 90°   **2** 45°   **3** 30°   **4** 60°.

Find the new time if the hour hand turns these angles from:

| 10 o'clock | | 5 o'clock |

How many degrees is the turn:

Clockwise ↻   Anti-clockwise ↺

5 90°   **9** 360°   **13** N to NE   **17** W to S
6 180°   **10** 90°   **14** NW to SE   **18** SE to NW
7 60°   **11** 30°   **15** SW to NW   **19** NE to NW
8 30°   **12** 180°   **16** E to SE?   **20** S to SE?

21 Place these angles in order of size, smallest first.

A   B   C   D

C

Combine set squares to make angles of:

1 135°   **2** 75°   **3** 120°   **4** 150°.

Find the new time if the hour hand turns these angles from:

| 4 o'clock | | 11 o'clock |

How many degrees is the turn:

Clockwise   Anti-clockwise

5 90°   **9** 180°   **13** S to SE   **17** N to SE
6 360°   **10** 30°   **14** SE to W   **18** NW to N
7 60°   **11** 270°   **15** NE to SE   **19** SW to SE
8 150°   **12** 120°   **16** W to S?   **20** E to NW?

Place the angles in each shape in order of size, smallest first.

21 **22** **23** **24**

25 What is the sum of the angles of a square?

26 What is the sum of the angles of:
   a) a set square   b) an equilateral triangle?

On these pages you will learn to use a Carroll diagram to sort shapes and numbers.

Example

8, 13, 17, 20, 22, 23, 27, 28

This Carroll diagram shows how the above numbers were sorted.

	odd	not odd
over 20	23 27	28 22
not over 20	17 13	8 20

A

1 Copy the Carroll diagram and use it to sort the numbers.

| 12 | 3 | 18 | 5 | 17 | 4 | 19 | 6 |

odd	not odd

2 Copy the Carroll diagram and write the letters in the correct places.

A   B   C   D

E   F   G   H

triangles	not triangles

3 Copy the Carroll diagram and use it to sort the numbers.

| 27 | 8 | 95 | 115 | 2 | 33 | 14 | 246 |

2-digit	not 2-digit

B

1 Copy the Carroll diagram and use it to sort the numbers.

| 31 | 87 | 54 | 48 | 96 | 65 |
| 22 | 78 | 45 | 16 | 53 | 37 |

	odd	not odd
over 50		
not over 50		

2 Copy the Carroll diagram and write the letters in the correct places.

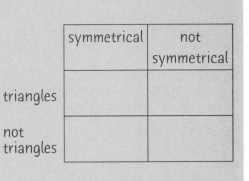

	symmetrical	not symmetrical
triangles		
not triangles		

C

1 Copy the Carroll diagram and use it to sort the numbers.

35	117	80	53
130	68	157	65
100	29	551	125

	2 digit nos.	not 2 digit nos.
multiples of 5		
not multiples of 5		

2 Copy the Carroll diagram and write the letters in the correct places.

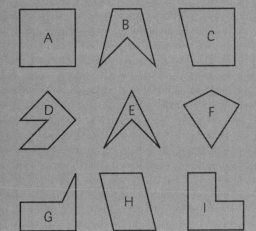

	concave	not concave
symmetrical		
not symmetrical		

On these pages you will learn to use Venn diagrams to sort shapes and numbers.

Example

Sort these numbers into a Venn diagram showing multiples of 3 and multiples of 5.

25   15   18   30   20   12

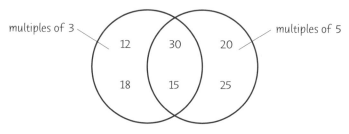

30 and 15 are multiples of both 3 and 5.
These numbers are put where the circles overlap.

A

1 Copy the Venn diagram and write the letters inside.

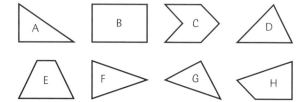

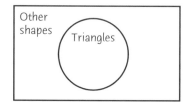

2 Copy the Venn diagram and sort these numbers by writing them in the right places.

14   25   10   15   20   8

Reminder:
the multiples of 2 are 2, 4, 6, 8, 10, 12 . . . .
the multiples of 5 are 5, 10, 15, 20, 25, ...

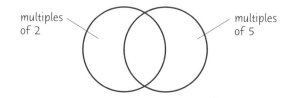

3 Copy the Venn diagram and sort these numbers by writing them in the right places.

3   18   15   147   39
94   36   7   23   64

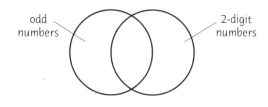

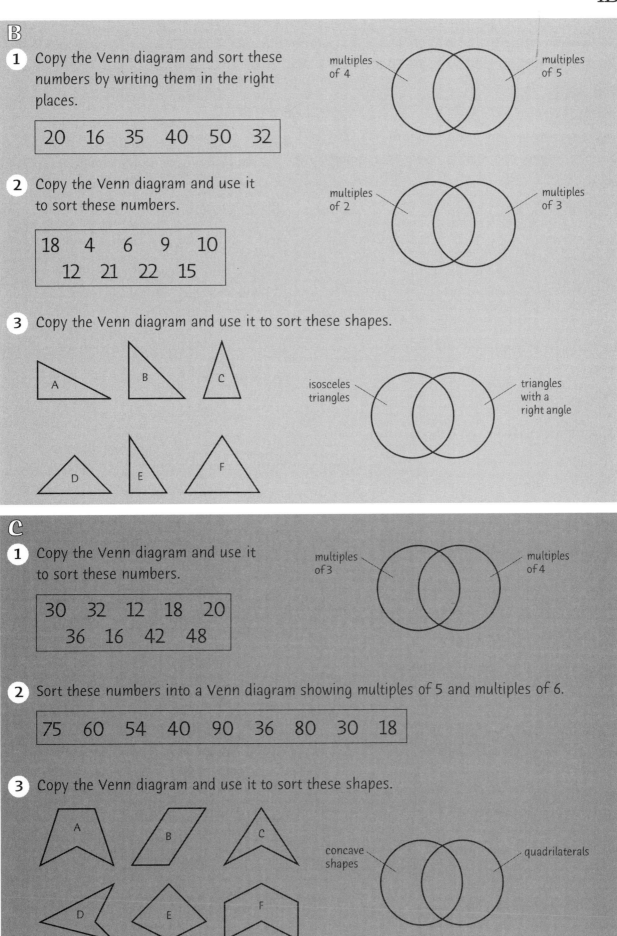

B

1 Copy the Venn diagram and sort these numbers by writing them in the right places.

| 20 | 16 | 35 | 40 | 50 | 32 |

multiples of 4   multiples of 5

2 Copy the Venn diagram and use it to sort these numbers.

| 18 | 4 | 6 | 9 | 10 |
| 12 | 21 | 22 | 15 |

multiples of 2   multiples of 3

3 Copy the Venn diagram and use it to sort these shapes.

A   B   C

D   E   F

isosceles triangles   triangles with a right angle

C

1 Copy the Venn diagram and use it to sort these numbers.

| 30 | 32 | 12 | 18 | 20 |
| 36 | 16 | 42 | 48 |

multiples of 3   multiples of 4

2 Sort these numbers into a Venn diagram showing multiples of 5 and multiples of 6.

| 75 | 60 | 54 | 40 | 90 | 36 | 80 | 30 | 18 |

3 Copy the Venn diagram and use it to sort these shapes.

A   B   C

D   E   F

concave shapes   quadrilaterals

On these pages you will learn to make and interpret a pictogram.

Example

A survey of trees in a wood found the following numbers of oak, ash, beech and elm trees.

B A B E O E B A E B
E E B A B E B O B A
O B A E A E O E B E
A E A O B O B A E B
E B B A E B E O A B

A tally chart showing the numbers of different trees.

Trees	Tally	Total
Ash	ⅢⅢ Ⅲ I	11
Beech	Ⅲ Ⅲ Ⅲ II	17
Elm	Ⅲ Ⅲ Ⅲ	15
Oak	Ⅲ II	7

The data in the tally chart can be shown in a pictogram.

Ash

Beech

Elm

Oak

 represents 2 trees.

A

1 The school football team scored these numbers of goals in their matches.

2 0 1 3 2 0 1 2
3 1 2 2 0 2 3 0
2 4 2 1 3 2 3 4

Make a tally chart and then draw a pictogram to show the results.

2 The pictogram shows the numbers of apples sold at playtime.

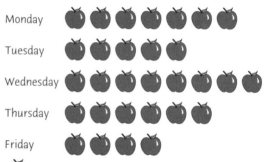

🍎 represents 2 apples.

a) How many apples were sold on Thursday?

b) How many apples were sold on Monday?

c) On which day were most apples sold?

d) On which day were least apples sold?

e) How many more apples were sold on Monday than on Tuesday?

f) How many fewer apples were sold on Tuesday than on Wednesday?

g) How many apples were sold during the week?

h) How many apples would need to be drawn on the pictogram if 24 apples were sold?

B

1. The days in February had the following numbers of hours of sunshine.

```
2  1  3  0  1  4  2
1  0  2  1  0  2  3
3  1  3  2  4  0  1
1  2  3  1  2  1  3
```

Make a tally chart and then draw a pictogram to show the results.

2. This pictogram shows the flavours of ice creams sold in a cafe.

represents 5 ice creams

a) How many coffee flavour ice creams were sold?

b) How many more vanilla flavour ice creams were sold than strawberry flavour?

c) Which was the most popular flavour?

d) Which was the least popular flavour?

e) How many ice creams were sold?

3. The next day ice cream sales were:

Chocolate	25
Vanilla	40
Coffee	35
Mint	20
Strawberry	30

Draw a pictogram to show the flavours sold.

C

1. A cafe sold bottles of orange, cola, lemonade and blackcurrant. In one day they sold the following bottles.

```
C  L  O  B  L  O  C  C  L  O
O  C  C  L  O  B  C  L  L  B
L  C  B  C  C  L  C  O  C  C
B  L  O  C  L  B  O  L  L  C
O  L  O  L  O  C  C  L  C  C
```

Make a tally chart and then draw a pictogram to show the results.

2. This pictogram shows the size of the audience for Toy Story.

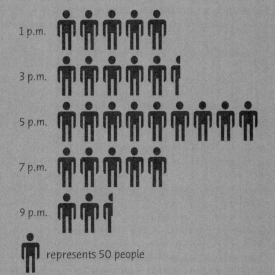

represents 50 people

a) How many people saw the 1 p.m. performance?

b) How many people saw the 9 p.m. performance?

c) How many more people saw the 3 p.m. performance than the 7 p.m. performance?

d) Which performance had the smallest audience? Explain why.

e) How many people saw the film during the day?

f) Do you think it was the weekend or a week day? Why?

On these pages you will learn:

- **to make a tally chart.**
- **to make and interpret a bar chart.**

Example

The ages of children in a Junior Rugby Club.

```
9   10   7    8    8    11   9    10
9   10   10   9    8    10   9    9
7    8   10   9    9    10   9    8
11   9    8   10   7    8    10   8
8    9   11   8    9    11   10   9
```

A tally chart showing the ages:

Age	Tally	Total
7 –	|||	3
8 –	||||| |||||	10
9 –	||||| ||||| |||	13
10 –	||||| |||||	10
11 –	||||	4

The ages in the tally chart can be displayed in a bar chart.

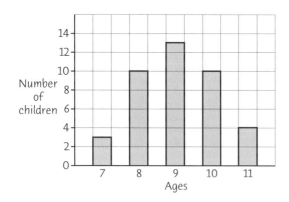

A

1 In their games lessons a class had played netball, football, rounders and hockey. At the end of the year they were asked to choose their favourite sport. These are the results.

```
N   F   R   H   R   F
H   N   F   R   F   N
H   F   H   N   F   H
F   F   R   F   H   N
```

Make a tally chart and then draw a bar chart to show the results.

2 The children in another class chose their favourite colours.

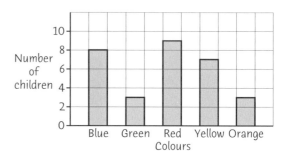

a) How many children chose blue?

b) How many children chose yellow?

c) Which colour was chosen most often?

d) Which colours were chosen least often?

e) How many more children chose blue than chose green?

f) How many fewer children chose orange than chose yellow?

g) How many children are there in this class?

h) Kevin says that over half the class chose red or yellow. Is he right? Explain why.

B

1 The children in 4Z were asked how many children were there in their family. These are the results:

```
2 3 1 2 4 3 1 2
3 4 2 3 1 5 3 2
2 1 2 5 3 2 2 3
2 3 4 1 2 3 2 1
```

Make a tally chart and then draw a bar chart to show the results.

2 This bar chart shows the number of vowels in the first page of a book.

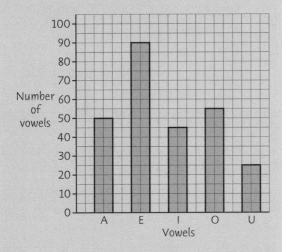

a) Which was the most common vowel?
b) Which was the least common vowel?
c) How many As were there?
d) How many Us were there?
e) Which letter appeared half as often as E?
f) How many more Os were there than Is?
g) How many vowels were there altogether?

3 Make a tally chart of the vowels in question 1 in Section A on page 116. Draw a bar chart to show the results.

C

1 John wanted to know how long the words were in his reading book. He found that in one passage the words had these numbers of letters:

```
3 3 4 4 4 3 7 4 2 2
2 7 2 6 2 8 2 2 4 5
2 7 5 2 3 4 6 3 5 2
3 5 7 2 2 7 4 3 5 6
5 3 2 8 2 4 6 7 3 4
```

Make a tally chart and then draw a bar chart to show the results.

2 This bar chart shows the number of diners at a restaurant.

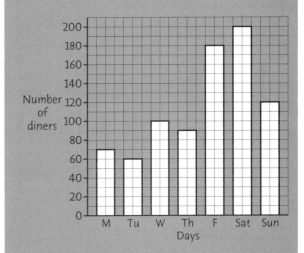

a) How many diners were there on Thursday?
b) How many more diners were there on Friday than on Monday?
c) Which day had the most diners? Explain why.
d) Which day had the least diners?
e) How many people dined at the restaurant during the week?

3 Make a tally chart of the lengths of the words in Section C on this page. Draw a bar chart to show the results.

Write in words.

1 308   **5** 2605

2 1297   **6** 3089

3 4362   **7** 5240

4 1500   **8** 8060

What is the value of the underlined digit?

9 2<u>6</u>13   **13** 33<u>8</u>6

10 157<u>0</u>   **14** <u>6</u>052

11 324<u>8</u>   **15** 793<u>4</u>

12 <u>5</u>861   **16** 9<u>5</u>29

Count on in 10s:

17 50 from 237

18 40 from 380

19 70 from 536

20 60 from 475.

Count on in 100s:

21 400 from 1831

22 800 from 2569

23 300 from 4924

24 700 from 3792.

Count back in 1000s:

25 6000 from 8235

26 3000 from 7810

27 5000 from 6497

28 4000 from 9063.

Multiply by 10.

29 148   **33** 25

30 53   **34** 781

31 217   **35** 690

32 570   **36** 436

Divide by 10.

37 2000   **41** 8610

38 3240   **42** 5000

39 390   **43** 1800

40 4700   **44** 6520

Write these numbers in order. Start with the smallest.

45 7981 7198 8197 8719

46 1782 2178 2187 1827

47 3649 3469 3694 3496

48 1573 1375 1735 1537

Estimate the numbers shown by the arrows.

49 0 ↓ ↓ 10

50 0 ↓ ↓ 20

51 0 ↓ ↓ 50

52 0 ↓ ↓ 100

Round to the nearest:

(10)   (100)

53 73   **57** 620

54 146   **58** 970

55 325   **59** 340

56 291   **60** 750

61 What number is shown by each arrow?

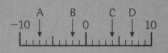

A   B   C D
−10 ↓   ↓ 0   ↓ ↓ 10

62 Which of these numbers are:
a) odd   b) even?

| 47 | 316 | 23 | 38 |
| 270 | 5 | 54 | 91 |

Write the first six multiples of:

63 10   **65** 4

64 6   **66** 9.

Write down the numbers in the box which are multiples of:

67 2   **69** 5

68 3   **70** 7.

| 14 | 15 | 18 | 20 |
| 21 | 35 | 49 | 60 |

What fraction of each shape is shaded?

1   **4**

2   **5**

3   **6**

Write the equivalent fractions shown by each pair.

7

8

9

10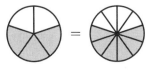

Copy and complete these equivalent fractions.
(You can use the fraction charts on page 20.)

11 $\frac{1}{4} = \frac{\square}{8}$ **15** $1 = \frac{\square}{10}$

12 $\frac{1}{2} = \frac{\square}{6}$ **16** $\frac{2}{3} = \frac{\square}{6}$

13 $1 = \frac{\square}{3}$ **17** $\frac{2}{5} = \frac{\square}{10}$

14 $\frac{1}{2} = \frac{\square}{10}$ **18** $1 = \frac{\square}{8}$

Find

19 $\frac{1}{2}$ of 30 **23** $\frac{1}{4}$ of 32

20 $\frac{1}{3}$ of 18 **24** $\frac{1}{10}$ of 60

21 $\frac{1}{5}$ of 40p **25** $\frac{1}{3}$ of £12

22 $\frac{1}{10}$ of 50 cm **26** $\frac{1}{2}$ of 1 m

What fraction of:

27 £1 is 50p **31** 1 m is 10 cm

28 £1 is 10p **32** 1 m is 50 cm

29 £1 is 25p **33** 1 m is 1 cm

30 £1 is 20p **34** 1 m is 25 cm.

Give the value of the underlined figure.

35 3·<u>2</u> **39** 2·<u>6</u>

36 1<u>6</u>·4 **40** 12<u>8</u>·3

37 0·<u>5</u> **41** <u>1</u>7·1

38 <u>1</u>9·7 **42** 13·<u>9</u>

Write as fractions.

43 0·1 **47** 0·5

44 0·25 **48** 0·8

45 0·6 **49** 0·75

46 0·3 **50** 0·7

Write as decimals.

51 $\frac{1}{2}$ **55** $\frac{4}{10}$

52 $\frac{2}{10}$ **56** $\frac{1}{4}$

53 1 **57** $\frac{3}{10}$

54 $\frac{9}{10}$ **58** $\frac{3}{4}$

59 Write the numbers shown by the arrows as decimal fractions.

Work out

60 0·4 + 0·3 **64** 0·8 − 0·5

61 0·2 + 0·7 **65** 0·7 − 0·2

62 1·3 + 0·5 **66** 1·5 − 0·4

63 1·1 + 0·6 **67** 1·9 − 0·3

Arrange in order. Start with the smallest.

68 1·5 5·1 2·4 4·2

69 3·8 8·8 8·3 3·3

70 54 5·4 4·5 45

71 7·9 9 7 9·7

72 6 16 1·6 6·1

Copy and complete.

1 $135 + 39 = \square$

2 $48 + 27 = \square$

3 $600 + \square = 1300$

4 $156 + \square = 200$

5 $\square + 40 = 151$

6 $\square + 76 = 119$

7 $82 - 38 = \square$

8 $500 - 64 = \square$

9 $204 - \square = 197$

10 $1000 - \square = 250$

11 $\square - 90 = 168$

12 $\square - 32 = 145$

Work out

13 $\begin{array}{r} 138 \\ + \ 91 \end{array}$ **17** $\begin{array}{r} 217 \\ - \ 81 \end{array}$

14 $\begin{array}{r} 257 \\ + \ 36 \end{array}$ **18** $\begin{array}{r} 390 \\ - \ 54 \end{array}$

15 $\begin{array}{r} 592 \\ + \ 57 \end{array}$ **19** $\begin{array}{r} 626 \\ - \ 64 \end{array}$

16 $\begin{array}{r} 326 \\ + \ 48 \end{array}$ **20** $\begin{array}{r} 583 \\ - \ 78 \end{array}$

Set out correctly and find the totals.

21 $4 + 37 + 246 + 25$

22 $54 + 123 + 9 + 16$

23 £3·73 + 65p + 48p

24 £1·26 + 57p + £2·43

Set out correctly and find the differences.

25 $137 - 66$

26 $392 - 58$

27 £4·18 − £1·45

28 £3·60 − £1·32

29 Sam buys a coat for £79 and a pair of shoes for £26. How much does she spend?

30 Emma's grandmother is 91. Emma is 35. What is the difference in their ages?

Copy and complete.

31 $23 \times 4 = \square$

32 $12 \times 11 = \square$

33 $8 \times \square = 32$

34 $6 \times \square = 0$

35 $\square \times 2 = 58$

36 $\square \times 7 = 35$

37 $48 \div 6 = \square$

38 $4000 \div 100 = \square$

39 $16 \div \square = 16$

40 $27 \div \square = 3$

41 $\square \div 10 = 600$

42 $\square \div 2 = 960$

Copy and complete.

43 $\begin{array}{r} 25 \\ \times \ 6 \end{array}$ **45** $\begin{array}{r} 34 \\ \times \ 9 \end{array}$

44 $\begin{array}{r} 63 \\ \times \ 8 \end{array}$ **46** $\begin{array}{r} 52 \\ \times \ 7 \end{array}$

Copy and complete.

47 $5\overline{)85}$ **49** $4\overline{)72}$

48 $6\overline{)90}$ **50** $7\overline{)98}$

Work out and give the remainder as a whole number.

51 $36 \div 5$ **53** $26 \div 3$

52 $165 \div 10$ **54** $27 \div 4$

Work out

55 £43 ÷ 2   **57** £33 ÷ 4

56 £67 ÷ 10   **58** £11 ÷ 5

59 There are 24 chocolates in each box. How many chocolates are there in five boxes?

60 The 92 children in Year 4 are divided into four equal teams. How many children are there in each team?

61 What is the product of 23 and 7?

62 Eight friends share the cost of a meal equally. The bill is for £132. How much should each person pay?

Copy and complete.

1. $100\,cm = \square\,m$
2. $\frac{1}{2}\,m = \square\,cm$
3. $\frac{1}{10}\,m = \square\,cm$
4. $25\,cm = \square\,m$
5. $1\,km = \square\,m$
6. $\frac{1}{10}\,km = \square\,m$

7. $500\,m = \square\,km$
8. $\frac{1}{10}\,cm = \square\,mm$
9. $10\,mm = \square\,cm$
10. $50\,mm = \square\,cm$
11. $1\,kg = \square\,g$
12. $2000\,g = \square\,kg$

13. $100\,g = \square\,kg$
14. $\frac{1}{2}\,kg = \square\,g$
15. $500\,ml = \square\,litre$
16. $4\,litres = \square\,ml$
17. $1000\,ml = \square\,litre$
18. $\frac{1}{10}\,litre = \square\,ml$

Work out the measurement shown by each arrow.

19.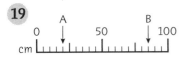
20.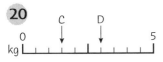
21. 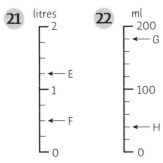 22.

23. A plank of wood is 2 metres long. 65 cm is sawn off. How long is the plank which is left?

24. There are ten coins in a pile. Each coin is 3 mm thick. How high is the pile in centimetres?

25. Four cans of peaches weigh 2 kilograms. What does each can weigh?

26. Anna makes one and a half litres of orange juice. She pours 700 ml into a bottle. How much is left?

27. What is the area of the rectangle?

28. What is the perimeter of the rectangle?

29. Use squared paper. Draw rectangles with areas of:
   a) $12\,cm^3$
   b) $15\,cm^2$.

30. Work out the perimeters of the rectangles you have drawn.

Copy and complete.

31. $5\,weeks = \square\,days$
32. $180\,seconds = \square\,minutes$
33. $30\,months = \square\,years$
34. $4\,hours = \square\,minutes$

35. $2\,days = \square\,hours$
36. $8\,decades = \square\,years$
37. $3\,years = \square\,weeks$
38. $90\,minutes = \square\,hours$

How many days are there in these months?

39. September
40. October
41. November
42. December

Write each time shown:
a) in words
b) in figures, using a.m. and p.m..

43. 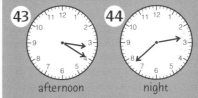 44.

afternoon   night

45. **8:51** 46. **6:14**
   morning   evening

47. The first lesson after playtime ends at 11:35. The lesson lasts for 50 minutes. At what time does playtime end?

48. The next lesson lasts 40 minutes. When does lunchtime begin?

Write the name of each of these 2-D shapes.

1

5

2

6

3

7

4

8

9 How many lines of symmetry does each of the above shapes have?

Use squared paper. Copy the shape and the mirror line and sketch the reflection.

10

13

11

14

12

15

Write the name of each of these 3-D shapes.

16   17

18

19 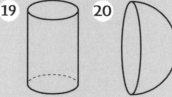   20

21

How many cubes are needed to build each of these shapes?

22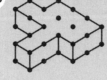

23

24 Give the co-ordinates of each letter.

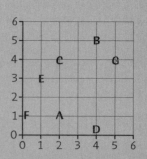

Look at the grid above. Which letter is found:

25 North of D

26 South West of B

27 West of G

28 North East of A

29 South East of E

30 North West of G?

How many degrees is the clockwise turn:

31 N to S

32 SE to SW

33 NE to E

34 SW to NE

35 W to NW?

Find the new time if the hour hand turns:

36 180° from 9 o'clock

37 90° from 4 o'clock

38 30° from 4 o'clock

39 360° from 8 o'clock

40 60° from 8 o'clock.

1 Copy the Carroll diagram and use it to sort these numbers.

92	7	150	81
126	74	15	219
63	4	58	300

	even	not even
2-digits		
not 2-digits		

2 Copy the Venn diagram and write the letters in the correct places.

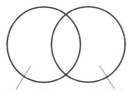

shapes with a right angle   quadrilaterals

3 The children in Class 4 were asked whether they walked to school, or came by bus, by car or by train.
These are the results:

```
W  B  C  W  W  T
C  W  B  W  C  W
B  W  T  C  W  B
W  C  W  B  C  W
B  W  W  C  W  C
```

Make a tally chart and then draw a pictogram to show the results.

4 This pictogram shows the number of children learning musical instruments at a school.

Guitar ♪ ♪ ♪ ♪
Piano ♪ ♪ ♪
Recorder ♪ ♪ ♪ ♪ ♪ ♪ ♪
Violin ♪ ♪ ♪

♪ represents 5 children

a) How many children were learning piano?
b) Which instrument was being learnt by most children?
c) How many more children were learning guitar than violin?
d) How many children were learning an instrument?

5 The diners at a canteen had a choice of eggs, fish, meat or salad. These are the meals chosen one lunchtime.

```
M  S  F  F  M  M
S  F  M  S  M  F
E  F  F  M  M  S
F  F  S  M  M  M
F  E  M  S  M  S
E  F  M  S  M  E
```

Make a tally chart and then draw a bar chart to show the results.

6 This bar chart shows the favourite colours of some children.

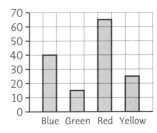

a) What was the most popular colour?
b) What was the least popular colour?
c) How many children chose yellow?
d) How many more children chose blue than chose green?
e) How many children were asked to choose their favourite colour?

Copy the crossnumber puzzles onto 1 cm squared paper.
Use the clues to solve the puzzles.

Clues across	Clues down
1 34 + 35	**1** 44 + 19
3 36 − 9	**2** 1000 − 49
5 75 − 40	**3** 23 × 10
6 6 × 5	**4** 700 ÷ 10
7 85 + 85	**8** 96 − 21
11 32 − 15	**9** 54 + 7
12 19 × 2	**10** 36 ÷ 2

B

Clues across	Clues down
1 28 ÷ 2	**1** 96 + 30
3 49 + 19	**2** 12 × 4
5 7 × 4	**3** 665 − 50
6 100 − 81	**4** 101 − 12
7 8·5 × 10	**7** 45 + 36
8 7 × 3	**8** 50 ÷ 2
10 30 ÷ 2	**9** 6 × 4
11 47 + 47	

C

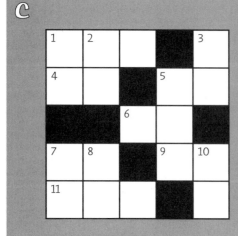

Clues across	Clues down
1 436 + 57	**1** 8 × 6
4 29 × 3	**2** 132 − 35
5 360 ÷ 4	**3** 0·6 × 100
6 9 × 8	**5** 37 × 25
7 113 − 44	**7** 9 × 7
9 6 × 9	**8** 460 ÷ 5
11 40 × 8	**10** 7^2

Check the answers by doing the inverse operation.

A

Copy and complete by writing the missing digits in the boxes.

1 $23 + \square 4 = 37$

2 $\square 1 + 25 = 56$

3 $3\square + \square 7 = 49$

4 $\square 6 + 19 = 35$

5 $4\square + \square 2 = 54$

6 $\square 8 + 33 = 61$

7 $4\square + 28 = 73$

8 $26 + 1\square = 41$

9 $46 - \square 3 = 13$

10 $\square 8 - 1\square = 21$

11 $5\square - \square 1 = 16$

12 $\square 2 - 35 = 7$

13 $6\square - \square 4 = 34$

14 $75 - 5\square = 18$

15 $3\square - \square 1 = 9$

16 $\square 1 - 3\square = 25$

B

Copy and complete by writing the missing digit in the boxes.

1
```
   □ 2
 + 2 □
 ─────
   5 9
```

2
```
   5 □
 + □ 1
 ─────
 1 1 4
```

3
```
   □ 5
 + 3 □
 ─────
   7 9
```

4
```
   5 □
 + 1 2
 ─────
   7 0
```

5
```
   □ 8
 + 3 8
 ─────
   9 6
```

6
```
   3 □
 + □ 6
 ─────
   6 3
```

7
```
   □ 8
 - 2 □
 ─────
   2 5
```

8
```
   6 □
 - □ 6
 ─────
   5 1
```

9
```
   □ 5
 - 3 9
 ─────
   3 6
```

10
```
   5 □
 - 2 8
 ─────
   2 9
```

11
```
   □ 2
 - 4 4
 ─────
   4 8
```

12
```
   4 □
 - □ 8
 ─────
   1 4
```

C

Copy and complete by writing the missing digits in the boxes.

1
```
   □ 3 □
 + 1 7 6
 ───────
   6 1 2
```

2
```
   3 □ 4
 + □ 9 8
 ───────
   6 5 2
```

3
```
   2 7 □
 + 1 □ 6
 ───────
   4 5 9
```

4
```
   3 □ 2
 - □ 5 □
 ───────
   2 1 1
```

5
```
   5 1 □
 - 2 □ 4
 ───────
   2 8 4
```

6
```
   2 □ 3
 - □ 7 5
 ───────
   1 1 8
```

7
```
   □ 4
 ×   3
 ─────
   7 □
```

8
```
   □ 2
 ×   5
 ─────
 1 6 □
```

9
```
   □ 9
 ×   6
 ─────
 1 7 □
```

10
```
   □ 9
 ×   6
 ─────
 1 7 □
```

11
```
   □ 7
 ×   4
 ─────
 2 6 □
```

12
```
   □ 3
 ×   8
 ─────
 1 8 □
```

TEST 1.

1. Write one thousand two hundred and thirty – eight in figures.

2. Round 452 to the nearest 100.

3. Add together 135 and 40.

4. How many quarters make one half.

5. What is the difference between 84 and 39?

6. How many centimetres are there in 2 metres?

7. What is the product of 7 and 4?

8. How many minutes are there in 3 hours?

9. Meena has one pound. She spends 42p. How much does she have left?

10. How many faces does a cube have?

11. Count on 6 from −2.

12. Write 0·3 as a fraction.

13. One litre of water is in a jug. 400 ml is poured out. How much water is left?

14. Write five to four in the afternoon in figures, using a.m. or p.m..

15. One book costs £6. What is the total cost of three books?

16. How many 5p coins make 40p?

17. Add 1·3 to 0·4.

18. One can weighs 400 g. What is the weight of five cans in kilograms?

19. How many degrees are there in two right-angles?

20. Write the first five multiples of 8.

TEST 2

1. What is the sum of 34 and 26?

2. How many fifths make one whole one?

3. The temperature is 3°C. It falls by 5°C. What is the new temperature?

4. Subtract 0·3 from 0·8.

5. How many days are there in 4 weeks?

6. What is the third multiple of 9?

7. Write two thousand and seventy-six in figures.

8. Divide 3160 by 10.

9. A dress costs £65. Zoe has £37. How much more does she need?

10. How many degrees are there in half a right-angle?

11. How many boxes of six can be made from 30 eggs?

12. A rope is 3 metres long. 60 cm is cut off. How long is the rope now?

13. From 97 take 41.

14. One ticket costs £3. How much do eight tickets cost?

15. Write 2000 grams in kilograms?

16. How many sides does a hexagon have?

17. What is double 280?

18. What is one quarter of 2 litres in millilitres?

19. A lesson starts at 10:55. It lasts 40 minutes. When does it finish?

20. What is one third of 60?

TEST 3.

1. What is the difference between 100 and 72?

2. Write eight tenths as a decimal.

3. How many seconds are there in two minutes?

4. Four pencils cost £1. How much does one cost?

5. Write the fifth multiple of 6.

6. How many metres is one and a quarter kilometres?

7. Add 1000 to 3756.

8. How many degrees is the turn from north to south?

9. Victor is 48. His son is one sixth of his age. How old is his son?

10. Write one thousand three hundred and nine in figures.

11. Subtract 64 from 85.

12. One tin costs 40p. What is the cost of five tins?

13. Half a litre of cola is shared equally between two glasses. How much is in each glass in millilitres?

14. What is the perimeter of a rectangle 6 cm by 4 cm?

15. Round 763 to the nearest 100.

16. What is the sum of 1·6 and 0·3?

17. Each cake weighs 200 g. What is the weight of ten cakes?

18. How many thirds make one whole one?

19. What number is halfway between 150 and 200?

20. Subtract the number of days in June from the number of days in this year.

TEST 4

1. What is the product of 9 and 5?

2. The temperature is −1°C. It rises 4°C. What is the new temperature?

3. Add together 57 and 38.

4. Four tennis balls cost £3. How much does one ball cost?

5. Write two and a half litres as millilitres.

6. Subtract three tenths from one whole one.

7. How many sides does a quadrilateral have?

8. What is one fifth of £20?

9. How many 7s make 28?

10. A plank is 2 metres long. 60 cm is sawn off. How much is left?

11. Multiply 8 by 4.

12. Dilip buys a paper for 35p. How much change should he have if he pays with a £2 coin?

13. Write five thousand and seven in figures.

14. A TV programme starts at 6:45 and finishes at 7:20. How long does the programme last?

15. What is the total of 400 and 273?

16. Find the new time if the hour hand turns 90° from 7 o'clock.

17. Take 6 away from 2000.

18. One parcel weighs 800 g. Another weighs half a kilogram. What is their combined weight.

19. Write one quarter as a decimal.

20. Fifty-six children are divided into 8 teams. How many children are there in each team?

How to learn a times table.

BY YOURSELF

1 Read the table over and over.

2 Cover the table and say it out loud or in your mind.

3 Say it more and more quickly.

4 Try to say the table backwards.

WITH A FRIEND

Ask each other questions like:

What is 6 times 4?

Multiply 4 by 7.

How many fours make 32?

Divide 36 by 4.

$1 \times 1 = 1$	$1 \times 2 = 2$	$1 \times 3 = 3$	$1 \times 4 = 4$	$1 \times 5 = 5$
$2 \times 1 = 2$	$2 \times 2 = 4$	$2 \times 3 = 6$	$2 \times 4 = 8$	$2 \times 5 = 10$
$3 \times 1 = 3$	$3 \times 2 = 6$	$3 \times 3 = 9$	$3 \times 4 = 12$	$3 \times 5 = 15$
$4 \times 1 = 4$	$4 \times 2 = 8$	$4 \times 3 = 12$	$4 \times 4 = 16$	$4 \times 5 = 20$
$5 \times 1 = 5$	$5 \times 2 = 10$	$5 \times 3 = 15$	$5 \times 4 = 20$	$5 \times 5 = 25$
$6 \times 1 = 6$	$6 \times 2 = 12$	$6 \times 3 = 18$	$6 \times 4 = 24$	$6 \times 5 = 30$
$7 \times 1 = 7$	$7 \times 2 = 14$	$7 \times 3 = 21$	$7 \times 4 = 28$	$7 \times 5 = 35$
$8 \times 1 = 8$	$8 \times 2 = 16$	$8 \times 3 = 24$	$8 \times 4 = 32$	$8 \times 5 = 40$
$9 \times 1 = 9$	$9 \times 2 = 18$	$9 \times 3 = 27$	$9 \times 4 = 36$	$9 \times 5 = 45$
$10 \times 1 = 10$	$10 \times 2 = 20$	$10 \times 3 = 30$	$10 \times 4 = 40$	$10 \times 5 = 50$

$1 \times 6 = 6$	$1 \times 7 = 7$	$1 \times 8 = 8$	$1 \times 9 = 9$	$1 \times 10 = 10$
$2 \times 6 = 12$	$2 \times 7 = 14$	$2 \times 8 = 16$	$2 \times 9 = 18$	$2 \times 10 = 20$
$3 \times 6 = 18$	$3 \times 7 = 21$	$3 \times 8 = 24$	$3 \times 9 = 27$	$3 \times 10 = 30$
$4 \times 6 = 24$	$4 \times 7 = 28$	$4 \times 8 = 32$	$4 \times 9 = 36$	$4 \times 10 = 40$
$5 \times 6 = 30$	$5 \times 7 = 35$	$5 \times 8 = 40$	$5 \times 9 = 45$	$5 \times 10 = 50$
$6 \times 6 = 36$	$6 \times 7 = 42$	$6 \times 8 = 48$	$6 \times 9 = 54$	$6 \times 10 = 60$
$7 \times 6 = 42$	$7 \times 7 = 49$	$7 \times 8 = 56$	$7 \times 9 = 63$	$7 \times 10 = 70$
$8 \times 6 = 48$	$8 \times 7 = 56$	$8 \times 8 = 64$	$8 \times 9 = 72$	$8 \times 10 = 80$
$9 \times 6 = 54$	$9 \times 7 = 63$	$9 \times 8 = 72$	$9 \times 9 = 81$	$9 \times 10 = 90$
$10 \times 6 = 60$	$10 \times 7 = 70$	$10 \times 8 = 80$	$10 \times 9 = 90$	$10 \times 10 = 100$